Praise for *Think Confident, Be Confident*

"In *Think Confident, Be Confident*, Drs. Sokol and Fox, two experienced and top-notch clinicians, give the reader an unfailingly encouraging, optimistic message: 'You *can* become a more confident person. You *can* reduce the role that self-doubt plays in your life. You *will* learn how to think and act in ways that will improve your life, starting today.' The book's caring, upbeat message, combined with its many exercises derived from evidence-based cognitive therapy, will provide readers with valuable new psychological skills that endure."
—Cory F. Newman, PhD, ABPP, Director of the Center for Cognitive Therapy

"*Think Confident, Be Confident* by Leslie Sokol and Marci Fox is a clear-thinking, helpful guide to putting your self-doubts behind you so you can get ahead with your life. Filled with practical and easy-to-follow techniques, you will find yourself changing old patterns of thinking to feel like new again."   —Robert L. Leahy, PhD, author of *Anxiety Free*

"Drs. Sokol and Fox draw upon the science of cognitive therapy to help lift readers out of doubt. *Think Confident, Be Confident* shows you how to use moments of self-doubt as fertile ground to develop lasting self-confidence. Doubt you can do it? Think again."
—Dennis Greenberger, PhD, and Christine A. Padesky, PhD, authors of *Mind Over Mood*

"Drs. Sokol and Fox provide a clear path from doubt to confidence, based on tried and true cognitive strategies that have been used for decades to transform negative thinking into realistic thinking. *Think Confident, Be Confident* is well written and the approach taken is straightforward and practical. This book will provide much-needed relief to those who struggle with unnecessary doubt!"
—Martin M. Antony, PhD, ABPP, author of *The Anti-Anxiety Workbook*

"Although doubt can have several positive forms (rational skepticism; 'reasonable doubt' in criminal cases), doubt can also undermine self-esteem, cripple effective decision-making, and in the extreme lead to anxiety and/or depression. *Think Confident, Be Confident* discusses the clinical aspects of doubt. Written by world-leading experts in cognitive therapy, but at an easily accessible level, this book is a definitive source for assessment and intervention with doubt. My prediction is that *Think Confident, Be Confident* will serve as *the* sourcebook in this area, and is recommended to anyone who works with patients who experience pathological or clinical doubt."
—Keith S. Dobson, PhD, President of the Academy of Cognitive Therapy

Think
CONFIDENT,
Be CONFIDENT

A Four-Step Program to Eliminate Doubt and Achieve Lifelong Self-Esteem

LESLIE SOKOL, PhD, and MARCI G. FOX, PhD

A PERIGEE BOOK

A PERIGEE BOOK
Published by the Penguin Group
Penguin Group (USA) Inc.
375 Hudson Street, New York, New York 10014, USA
Penguin Group (Canada), 90 Eglinton Avenue East, Suite 700, Toronto, Ontario M4P 2Y3, Canada
(a division of Pearson Penguin Canada Inc.)
Penguin Books Ltd., 80 Strand, London WC2R 0RL, England
Penguin Group Ireland, 25 St. Stephen's Green, Dublin 2, Ireland (a division of Penguin Books Ltd.)
Penguin Group (Australia), 250 Camberwell Road, Camberwell, Victoria 3124, Australia
(a division of Pearson Australia Group Pty. Ltd.)
Penguin Books India Pvt. Ltd., 11 Community Centre, Panchsheel Park, New Delhi—110 017, India
Penguin Group (NZ), 67 Apollo Drive, Rosedale, North Shore 0632, New Zealand
(a division of Pearson New Zealand Ltd.)
Penguin Books (South Africa) (Pty.) Ltd., 24 Sturdee Avenue, Rosebank, Johannesburg 2196,
South Africa

Penguin Books Ltd., Registered Offices: 80 Strand, London WC2R 0RL, England

While the author has made every effort to provide accurate telephone numbers and Internet addresses at the time of publication, neither the publisher nor the author assumes any responsibility for errors, or for changes that occur after publication. Further, the publisher does not have any control over and does not assume any responsibility for author or third-party websites or their content.

First edition: October 2009

Library of Congress Cataloging-in-Publication Data

Sokol, Leslie.
   Think confident, be confident : a four-step program to eliminate doubt and achieve lifelong self-esteem / Leslie Sokol and Marci G. Fox.
      p. cm.
   "A perigee book."
   Includes index.
   ISBN 978-0-399-53529-1
  1. Self-doubt.   2. Self-esteem.   3. Self-confidence.   I. Fox, Marci G.   II. Title.
   BF697.5.S428.S65 2009
   158.1—dc22   2009014077

PRINTED IN THE UNITED STATES OF AMERICA

10 9 8 7 6 5 4 3 2 1

Most Perigee books are available at special quantity discounts for bulk purchases for sales promotions, premiums, fund-raising, or educational use. Special books, or book excerpts, can also be created to fit specific needs. For details, write: Special Markets, Penguin Group (USA) Inc., 375 Hudson Street, New York, New York 10014.

Dedicated to Aaron T. Beck, MD, and Judith S. Beck, PhD,
champions of cognitive therapy

CONTENTS

Step 4
Take Action

FOREWORD

Self-doubt is part of the human condition, but in excess, it under-mines individuals' confidence and interferes with their ability to set and work toward goals that are important to them: in produc-tive activities (such as work, home management, sports, leisure pursuits) and in relationships (platonic and romantic, with friends, family, neighbors, and coworkers). Self-doubt inhibits affirmative action and leads to unnecessary distress, suffering, and avoidance.

Fortunately, *Think Confident, Be Confident* provides a solution to the problem. It was written by two of our associates, who have been with us for many years. Dr. Sokol is the director of education for the Beck Institute for Cognitive Therapy and Research and Dr. Fox is a senior faculty member in our Extramural Training Program. They have made incalculable contributions to the field of cogni-tive therapy in the past twenty-five years through clinical care and teaching and supervising thousands of clinicians worldwide. Drs. Sokol and Fox provide answers to two essential questions: Why do people have self-doubt? What can they do to improve their lives? They explain the origins of self-doubt, differentiate between real-istic concern (which can be helpful) and excessive doubt (which can cripple one's ability to take important action). Then they spell out how to use cognitive therapy techniques to quell unwarranted self-doubt and increase self-confidence.

Cognitive therapy, a time-limited form of talk therapy, has been shown to be remarkably effective in helping people with their psychological problems. One important strategy is learning how to respond to unrealistic thinking. When individuals are plagued with self-doubt, they often have inaccurate ideas about themselves ("I'm incompetent"; "I'm unlovable") and they negatively predict others' reactions or misperceive how others are viewing them ("He thought I did a poor job"; "She won't want to see me again").

But changing one's *thinking* is not enough. *Think Confident, Be Confident* also guides readers in how to change their *behavior* so they can begin to take reasonable social-, work-, or productivity-related actions they have been avoiding, believing their shortcomings would be exposed. It also helps readers recognize their accomplishments when they do take action, teaching them to give themselves credit instead of engaging in second-guessing and self-criticism.

Think Confident, Be Confident offers a unique, interactive four-step program. The authors have used their considerable clinical experience and expertise to develop practical, effective, problem-solving strategies. In Step 1, Label It, readers recognize and label their self-doubts. In Step 2, Question It, readers learn to examine the validity of their doubt. Step 3, Rethink It, helps readers replace their doubt-driven rules and strategies with more productive ones and create more accurate beliefs about the self. In Step 4, Take Action, readers learn to think and behave more effectively so they can reach their goals.

This book is an invaluable guide to both consumers and the professionals who treat them. It will reduce unwarranted self-doubt, increase self-confidence, and—most important—allow individuals to achieve their goals.

Judith S. Beck, PhD
Director, Beck Institute for Cognitive Therapy and Research
Clinical Associate Professor of Psychology in Psychiatry
University of Pennsylvania

Aaron T. Beck, MD
University Professor Emeritus of Psychiatry
University of Pennsylvania
President, Beck Institute for Cognitive Therapy and Research

INTRODUCTION

Imagine that you have made plans to meet friends at a restaurant. You arrive to find them at the bar engrossed in their conversations. You would like to rush over and say hello, but you don't. Instead you slowly approach the group and wait quietly for someone to ask you to join in.

Envision this work situation: You are about to address a meeting of your sales team. The agenda is a newly created project of yours, one in which you passionately believe. You look around at your team members and suddenly lose focus. Your plan of action feels as if it were riddled with holes. In your mind, you highlight the few negative comments coworkers have made to you about getting this project off the ground, and you forget about all the positive feedback you have received.

Think about an upcoming tennis match. Rather than being able to concentrate or have fun, you become fixated on your opponent's lightning-fast serve. Instead of being in the moment, using your well-practiced stroke and reflexes to effectively return those serves, you choke.

The underlying theme in all three of these situations is *doubt*.

Doubt makes you your own worst enemy. Instead of casually saying hello, believing in your plan, or returning the serve, you crumble. Doubt undermines your confidence.

If you've picked up this book, you have already taken the first step toward ending the relentless cycle of second-guessing yourself. Perhaps you can already envision how much better your life will become when you squash the doubts you have about yourself and build your confidence. *Think Confident, Be Confident* will help you to turn that vision into a reality. Let's take a look at how we can accomplish this.

We often don't recognize the enormous role doubt plays in our moods, actions, internal arousal, and motivation. Its effects are huge. However, it need not stop you in your tracks. Doubt is removable. You can be free to join the conversation, make decisions, reach for your goals, and enjoy the moment. To do so, you will have to learn to recognize doubt, face it, and remove it.

Doubt causes us problems because it is actually a *false alarm* going off in our body. The false alarm is ringing because we believe we are not prepared, skilled, or fortified when we actually are equipped. Doubt is a needless barrier to success. It comes from failing to recognize our strengths and exaggerating our weaknesses. We call this the false alarm. It is time to learn how to turn off the too easily tripped, malfunctioning false alarm.

There is a difference between realistic concern and doubt, however. Realistic concern is the increased apprehension we experience that cautions us to examine the specific situation and to evaluate if we are indeed prepared for it. Realistic concern is focused on a particular situation, is credible, and is warranted. It is a warning signal to take appropriate action. We'll train you to recognize the difference.

In this book, we will teach you how to squash crippling doubt and replace it with confidence. Our program is based on our success with thousands of people over the last thirty combined years as clinical psychologists with extremely active practices and training schedules. Rather than waiting to be the person you hope to become, we'll show you how you can *be* that person today. Our step-by-step approach will lead you to success, better relationships, and better performance.

How Cognitive Therapy Can Help

Practiced all over the world, cognitive therapy is a psychotherapeutic approach that follows this basic rule: *How we think influences how we feel and how we behave.* It has been proven in hundreds of clinical trials to be effective for a wide variety of issues and has been used in businesses to increase productivity, satisfaction, communication, and reduce stress and in schools to increase optimism, curb problem behavior, and diminish fear and sadness. Cognitive therapy has served as a powerful and effective self-help tool in combating issues such as depression, anxiety, phobias, overeating, anger, and relationship issues.

The cognitive model begins with our thoughts. This means that if we want to change our behavior and our emotional responses, we can do so by changing our thinking. Most individuals unconditionally accept their thoughts as true. Perceptions, though, are not always accurate. In this case, when thoughts are not true, we teach people to recognize the errors in their thinking so that those thoughts don't affect the way they feel, respond, and behave. When their thoughts are true, we help people use those thoughts to improve their decision-making, problem-solving, and coping skills.

Who We Are

As licensed psychologists with active private practices, we both provide training/teaching in cognitive therapy: Dr. Sokol through her work as director of education at the internationally acclaimed Beck Institute for Cognitive Therapy and Research, and Dr. Fox as a senior faculty member in the extramural training program, also at the Beck Institute.

Early on in our work together, we recognized that self-doubt is a critical area of patient care that is not comprehensively addressed. Often, it can play a role in the cause or exacerbation of people's difficulties. As a result, we developed our own program for working with people to reduce and replace doubt with a more realistic confident sense of self. The result was that clients often left our offices feeling more empowered. We also began training other mental health professionals by educating them on systematically reducing self-doubt and replacing it with self-confidence while teaching them cognitive therapy.

In this book, we bring our program to you.

What Our Book Will Help You Do

Our book is a unique, interactive, effective, cognitive therapy–based program that will teach you to conquer doubt, build true confidence, and develop lifelong self-esteem. Doubt will no longer cripple you. With our confidence-building method, you will truly believe in yourself no matter what situation presents itself. You will be able to reach your full potential rather than living unfulfilled or just status quo.

How to Use This Book

Our program is broken down into four steps. The first step is to **label your doubt**. Here we help you figure out what makes you tick—and what makes you most vulnerable to self-doubt. We uncover what your buttons are *before* they get pushed. Each of us has different vulnerabilities based on how doubt effects our interpretations of various situations.

What are you saying to yourself? Using a series of quizzes, we'll help you understand the main self-doubt labels that are causing your distress. Throughout this process, we also will share with you our own personal experiences as well as stories of others with whom we've worked.

The second step is to **question your doubt**. Rather than walking around impaired because you are simply accepting all the self-doubts that fill your head, you can begin to examine how accurate those self-doubts really are. You will learn how to realistically appraise these doubt messages, and instead of following them blindly, you will begin to use your resources. You will also learn how many of us unknowingly choose information that fits the insecure way we think about ourselves. When we do, we end up knocking our confidence and are biased against ourselves. Step two of the program will help you remove the bias and see things more realistically and positively.

In step three, we help you **rethink doubt**. You will learn what self-limiting, self-produced regulations you often unknowingly live by. We call them *if/then messages*. That is, *if* I do this, *then* something specific will happen that will either protect me from doubt or activate it. For example, "If I do everything perfectly, then I'll succeed or people will like me." "If I'm not perfect, then I'm a failure or people won't like me." Over time our if/then messages become rules—self-limiting, internal guiding principles that gradually restrict our lives and limit our positive thinking, experiences, and feelings. We essentially end up putting ourselves in a double-bind with these negative rules because they make us more vulnerable to self-doubt and limit our ability to have self-confidence. Through quizzes, exercises, and examples, we'll help you understand what your own if/then messages and rules are, and we'll show you how to replace them with realistic assumptions so that you can stop limiting your own effectiveness and success. We then work on helping you name and chip away at your doubt label so that you can replace it with a more confident and accurate belief.

Take action is the last step of the program. In this step we'll teach you specific, time-tested, easy-to-use skills based on the principles of cognitive therapy to squash doubt and then help you build and maintain your newfound confidence for lifelong self-esteem. These tools will allow you to enter the race rather than quit before you start. It means believing in yourself and not depending on anyone else to give you the recognition you can give yourself. Knowing you can count on yourself means that you can courageously tackle any situation. All of this is possible when you learn to live with no doubt.

Our Book Is Interactive

This book is designed to be interactive so that you can apply the material directly to yourself. Please feel free to write in the book. As you read and work through each step, there are quizzes and exercises for you to complete. Don't hesitate to write in the margins or use a separate notebook to take notes. Actively participating in the quizzes and exercises will make the program more effective for you.

Think
CONFIDENT,
Be CONFIDENT

Step 1
Label It

Chapter One

What Makes You Tick?

Doubt lurks in all of us. Jamie, a fifty-three-year-old physician, claims she has no doubt. "I don't really care if people like me or not," she maintains. Yet she is adored by her family and goes out of her way to show her love and commitment to them. Being loved and valued are things she takes for granted. It does not define who she is. Jamie is defined by her accomplishments. What makes her feel good about herself is her successes, but it is in that domain that her doubt waits.

Jamie has been a devoted and hardworking member of a prestigious and powerful board for the past fifteen years. The new chairman is trying to evict the longstanding members, like Jamie, off the board. Jamie is rattled and willing to fight to not let this happen. It is perfectly clear that the newly appointed young chairman has political reasons for his agenda. Yet Jamie wonders if this man thinks she has lost her edge and thus wants her off the board. Jamie's doubt has surfaced. Hiding in the background of her usually dominant confidence is the belief that maybe she is not good enough.

Doubt is always inside of us waiting for stress to push it to the surface. For some of us, doubt whispers in our ear. For others, doubt screams. Regardless, *once doubt surfaces, it colors how we think, how we feel, and how we act.*

There is an obstacle in your path. Do you set about trying to move it? Do you stop and ask yourself why you might actually want to do so? Do you tell yourself you don't deserve to remove it from your path? Do you get angry? Do you just walk away? One of these strategies is yours, which depends on how you respond to your self-doubt.

In this book, you will learn to recognize doubt and to understand how pervasively it shapes the way you view the world and how you feel, how you physically respond, and what you do. Understanding these components will give you the tools you need to courageously and freely make decisions and choices to achieve in all spheres of your life.

Realistic Concern Is Different from Doubt

Realistic concern is a warning signal alerting us to danger. It cautions us to take stock of a situation and evaluate if we are indeed equipped to handle it. For instance, you are a talented skateboarder and a fearless ice skater. You have decided to take up skiing. You buy yourself a warm outfit; rent yourself some skis; and, with a friend who knows the trails, head to the slopes. You ride the chairlift to the top of the trail, wiggle off the chair, and fall flat on your face. As you struggle to stand up, you think, "This isn't like other sports. I'm never going to make it down the mountain. I don't know what I'm doing." Your friend has already started down the slope without you, having assumed you would be close behind.

The concern inside you grows. You somewhat clumsily make your way down the mountain and then go get a lesson. Your concern in this case was right on target and warranted. It alerted you to the fact that you were not adequately prepared. This kind of realistic concern is grounded in reality, temporary and helpful.

Doubt is the enemy within that causes you to question your capability and desirability. It is unhelpful because it comes from unwarranted fear and leads you to conclude that you can't handle things when you can or that you are not desirable when the facts show otherwise. This *global unfounded doubt* is exactly what this book will teach you to turn off. The following two exercises will help you recognize when unrealistic global doubt is operating.

DOUBT TEST 1

Imagine for this exercise that you just got a great job in your area of expertise. It is the night before you begin the new job, and you are aware of feeling apprehensive. Answer yes or no to the following questions in accordance with what you feel is your characteristic way of thinking.

1. I have the technical skills necessary for this job.   __ Yes __ No

2. My past experiences helped equip me for this job.   __ Yes __ No

3. I catch on quickly enough.   __ Yes __ No

4. I'm willing to ask questions if I need help.   __ Yes __ No

5. If I face a problem, I'll be able to figure out what to do. __ Yes __ No

6. I can appear calm even if I'm not.   __ Yes __ No

7. I'm equipped with the brains to do this job.   __ Yes __ No

SELF-ANALYSIS

Did you answer yes to at least five of the seven questions? If you answered yes, then your mental picture is of being capable. There is no reason to have doubt. Doubt, in this scenario, is unrealistic and unwarranted.

Did you answer no to at least five of the seven questions? If you answered no, then you are experiencing doubt in response to the imagined situation. Your doubt leads you to unrealistically question your expertise and skill. Realistic concern is not actually necessary because this is your area of expertise, and you are equipped to handle the situation.

DOUBT TEST 2

For this exercise, imagine you are going to a big social event tonight with your significant other. Your significant other will know many of the people there but you will not. You notice you are feeling uneasy about going. Answer yes or no to the following questions.

1. If you had to, you could talk to anyone.   __ Yes __ No

2. You have interests you could talk about.   __ Yes __ No

3. You know how to make yourself presentable.   __ Yes __ No

4. You can be a good listener, letting others talk
   about themselves.   __ Yes __ No

5. Your significant other enjoys your company and
   will include you in conversations.   __ Yes __ No

6. You can think of things at the party to look
   forward to.   __ Yes __ No

7. You know you can be entertaining if you want to be.   __ Yes __ No

SELF-ANALYSIS

Did you answer yes to at least five of the seven questions? If so, you recognize doubt is unrealistic and unwarranted in this scenario. There is no good reason to be apprehensive as you picture yourself smiling and actively engaging in a conversation.

Did you answer no to at least five of the seven questions? If so, you are experiencing doubt. You are imagining yourself being socially undesirable and picture yourself struggling in conversations or spending much of your time being ignored by others. You fail to envision that you have the assets that make you socially desirable. Realistic concern is not really warranted and would be exaggerating any possible social shortcoming or awkwardness in this situation.

Learn to Differentiate Realistic Concern from Doubt

As you can see from the two tests, you can needlessly cause yourself stress when you let doubt get the best of you. Recognizing this useless, unwarranted doubt is the first step. Sometimes, however, our doubt is actually realistic concern. Realistic concern means you are not equipped to handle the situation, and you should take appropriate action to gain the necessary skills or to ask for help. Ignoring realistic concern can be risky. By not attending to realistic concern, you might put yourself in situations where your well-being, safety, or livelihood is compromised. Therefore, the second step is to differentiate realistic concern from doubt. If it's realistic concern, we'll teach you to take appropriate action. If it's doubt, we'll teach you through our program to squash it while building confidence. Use the following quiz to differentiate realistic concern from doubt.

REALISTIC CONCERN VS. DOUBT QUIZ

1. You've decided to go to a tropical paradise with eight of your friends. Most of your friends are certified divers and have organized a dive trip. You have had two hours of instruction in the hotel pool, and the dive instructor has told you that he will escort you on the trip.

   A. You fear harm will come to you and decline the offer. Although the dive instructor will accompany you, you feel you have not learned enough to be comfortable.

   B. You join your friends and go, hoping you'll be okay.

   C. You decline the offer out of fear, blaming your inadequacy.

2. A good friend offers you the opportunity to invest in her new business. She promises great return on your money, and other friends appear interested.

   A. You recognize you lack the necessary facts to make an informed decision and decline the offer; you are also thinking that in the present economic environment any business venture would be too risky.

   B. You write out a check immediately, and hope for the best.

   C. You decline the offer, and call yourself a wimp.

SELF-ANALYSIS

If you answered A in either example, you recognized that realistic concern was warranted. In both situations, real threat existed. Choosing to decline the dive or the investment was a reasonable choice.

If you chose B in either example, you chose to put yourself at risk, potentially to your detriment.

If you chose C in either situation, doubt took over. Instead of recognizing that realistic concern led you to decline the offers, you believed your doubt.

This quiz demonstrates that taking appropriate action requires differentiating realistic concern from doubt. You can use these questions in your daily life when you notice you are feeling concerned, distressed, or overwhelmed to help you differentiate realistic concern from doubt.

Here are the steps for differentiating realistic concern from doubt in your daily life:

1. The next time you are distressed, label the situation that is directly connected to your distress. Some examples are starting a new job, going back to school, getting a speeding ticket, getting on a plane, making an investment, and getting ready to go out on a Saturday night.

2. Assess your resources to help you differentiate whether you are experiencing appropriate realistic concern or doubt. Ask yourself, "Do I have the experience/skills I need?" Determine whether you have the required technical skills, experience, patience, or willingness to learn. Check if you have interests and opinions to share or know how to put yourself together. See if you are in fact equipped to face the situation.

3. Take appropriate action.

IF IT IS A REALISTIC CONCERN, THEN I SHOULD...	IF IT IS DOUBT, THEN I SHOULD...
Gain information, skill, or experience.	Just do it, take action, get started. Start the new job, go back to school, pay my speeding ticket, get on the plane, make the investment, or go out Saturday night.

Differentiating realistic concern from doubt is a necessary step in overcoming doubt. If you discover that your concern is unrealistic and yet continue to let it get in your way, you will be sacrificing confidence and paying the price for letting doubt take over. By questioning your competency or desirability or both you allow doubt to stop you from taking effective action.

The Doubt Pattern

Let's take a closer look at how doubt enters the picture. It's helpful to first become aware of how you are interpreting what's going on outside in the environment as well as inside your body. After that, you are going to become skilled at recognizing when doubt is talking to you, evaluating its legitimacy, and adopting more positive views of yourself. Looking at yourself through the lens of confidence will help you make beneficial rules for action and engage in constructive behaviors.

The Doubt Model

A typical pattern of doubt, presented through an example, is shown in the following list. As an exercise, think of the last time you noticed a significant shift in your mood or uncomfortable response in your body. Think back to the situation and see if it follows the doubt model.

Person Faces a Situation
(Friends cancel plans with you.)

Self-Doubt Is Activated
(You think, "I'm a loser.")

Negative Emotions Arise
(You feel disappointment, sadness, frustration, and/or irritation.)

The Situation Is Now Seen through the Lens of Doubt
(You think, "They probably have something better to do. I guess I don't matter as much as I thought. Maybe I'm not much fun to be with.")

Negative Emotions Increase and/or Continue
(You feel more disappointment, sadness, frustration, and/or irritation.)

Doubt-Driven Actions
(You open the fridge or a bottle of wine or crawl into bed.)

Doubt Is Affirmed
(You think, "I am a loser.")

Rules Develop to Survive the Doubt
(You think, "Next time, I'll think twice about making plans for fear of being disappointed.")

↓

Behaviors Result
(You have no future plans.)

↓

Self-Doubt Is Confirmed
(You think, "I am a loser.")

Triggers: How It All Begins

At any given moment of the day each of us is exposed to a multitude of external and internal experiences. *External stimuli* are those things going on around us. *Internal stimuli* are the sensations that we experience inside our bodies or minds. Both sets of experiences can set off doubt.

Just stop reading for a moment and try to be aware of everything going on in your environment. Where are you? What do you see? Are you alone or with others? What do you hear? Is it quiet or do you hear other people conversing or a baby crying or children playing or people arguing or laughing? Do you hear the television or the news or the radio? Is it dark or light? Maybe you see the glare of the sun through the window shades. Take a moment and mentally list the external sensations you are experiencing.

How we process these experiences is influenced by our underlying self-doubt. Do we see them in a neutral way or as a sign of danger or distress? Take the external trigger of overhearing two men arguing. One person may think nothing of the heated conversation; it may be a trigger for another, who may fear for his or her own safety; and still another may be concerned for the well-being of one of the men.

Internal stimuli are the thoughts and images that run through our head or the bodily sensations we experience. Thoughts can be spontaneous and bizarre, like the thought of flinging yourself off a tall building. They can be negative, like the thought of growing old and suffering in pain. Or they can be positive, like the thought of becoming wealthy. Thoughts can also be scary, like thinking you forgot where you put a valuable item. Images, like thoughts, are internal stimuli that arise unexpectedly. Thoughts and images appear unprompted and unplanned. They often either go unnoticed or are given more weight than they deserve.

Physical feelings are bodily sensations. Sit quietly for a moment and try to scan your body from the top of your head to your toes. Do you feel relaxed? Are you clenching your jaw? Is your mouth dry? Do your shoulders feel tight? Is your heart pounding? Do you have indigestion? Do you feel nauseous or have butterflies in your stomach? Do you notice shakiness or restlessness? Are you tired or full of energy? These are just a few of the sensations we experience in our bodies at any given time.

Feelings themselves are stimuli. The feelings of being bored, lonely, happy, excited, angry, overwhelmed, sad, or fearful are just a few examples. The more we focus on our feelings the more magnified those feelings become.

Stimuli, external or internal, are just that, stimuli. The thought or image of hurting someone might cross your mind, and you can either dismiss it as a silly intrusion or it can become a trigger to make you fear that you will in fact hurt someone. Consider the internal stimulus of feeling your heart racing. One person might perceive it as a sign of physical danger, another might see it as an opportunity to get energized, and another as a reprieve from hunger. Or consider suddenly feeling sad. You might think this is a sign of more sadness to come, another might see it as making sense based on the situation, and yet another may think nothing of it. It is our perceptions of those stimuli that create our trouble, and it is our self-doubt that shapes that perception.

Self-Doubt Enters the Picture

Every one of us perceives the world through a different lens. Our lenses are often colored by self-doubt. At some point or another, all of us find ourselves seeing the world through the lens of doubt. When doubt is biasing our perspective, we suffer needlessly. Those of us who allow doubt to be our filter suffer more than others. The first step in removing that filter of doubt is learning to recognize and label the doubt that has warped our perspective.

Imagine you have a fourteen-year-old son who is tall for his age and has large, well-defined muscles. His bulging arms and six-pack stomach are the admiration of others. A friend says to you, "Where did he get those genes?" You revel in the admiration your son is receiving. What if, instead, you heard that as a slight? You immediately shrink and feel insulted and wonder why your friend cannot see how your son looks like you did once, albeit thirty years ago. Through the lens of self-doubt, the compliment has become an insult.

Take an example from the tennis court. A husband and wife are avid tennis players. They play in a coed drill on Sunday mornings with some very aggressive, wisecracking men. One man in particular likes to compliment the wife's game and give her husband a hard time. If the husband is this man's partner and is standing at the net and he lets a ball get by him, this man will tell him, "You're not up there just to look good." The husband feels diminished and thinks, "I'm not that good." The reality is the husband is as good a player as the rest of them, but the underlying doubt of himself as an athlete leads him to perceive the bantering as an insult.

We are each vulnerable to different types of situations. For example, you might react differently from someone else when in one of these situations: a family member being short over the phone, a disagreement, receiving constructive criticism at work, being corrected, needing help, or making a mistake How we react to such triggers determines the degree of stress we experience.

Imagine you reach down to adjust the temperature in your car, and you are startled by a loud honk. You realize the light has turned green and proceed through the intersection. Glancing in your rearview mirror, you notice the person driving the car behind you is mouthing a complaint. Do you shrug it off, ignore it, and think nothing more about it? Or do you feel bad or embarrassed that you weren't paying attention? You might even believe you are dumb, irresponsible, or careless. You can let this situation activate your insecurity or you can tell yourself it's no big deal and in no way a reflection of your intellect, sensibility, or consideration for others that you missed the changing of the light. Do you let minor events like this activate doubt?

As you work though the program in *Think Confident, Be Confident*, you will learn to notice when doubt starts talking to you. External and internal sensations are simply that, until you subjectively interpret them. Your spin on an event is rarely the same as another's understanding of it. Have you ever noticed that your interpretation of a situation was not the same as someone else's who witnessed the same event? Have you ever wondered why you might have reacted so strongly, while your spouse took it in stride? We all have vulnerabilities, also known as *doubt triggers*.

DOUBT TEST 3

Imagine yourself in each of these scenarios. What's going through your mind? Take a moment to record your thoughts next to each item.

1. Your colleague walked into the office and did not say hello to you.

2. Your boss calls to tell you he wants to meet with you later today.

3. Your friend cancels lunch with no explanation as to why.

4. You don't get invited to a neighbor's holiday party.

5. You need to call someone for help because she has more expertise in what you're working on.

6. You'll be late on a deadline.

7. A friend is upset with you.

8. A family member is angry at you.

9. You get lost and will be late for a meeting.

10. The person you are talking to looks at her watch.

SELF-ANALYSIS

Which situations lead to emotional distress? Think about a family member being mad at you. Did you take it in stride knowing it will blow over or did you have an extreme reaction worrying that you will never be forgiven? Are you able to see this interaction as a typical pattern in his or her behavior and not a reflection of you? Strong negative reactions are caused by underlying doubt. Doubting our lovability leads us to fear rejection at every mishap.

In the second situation, your boss asking to meet with you, all kinds of thoughts are possible. It can be overwhelming to imagine, "What kind of trouble am I in?" A person who doubts his or her competence would be more likely to have such a thought. The confident person would think, "I've got some free time later this afternoon so I'll talk to him then." She feels neutral, knowing she can handle whatever problem has arisen. Are you beginning to become aware that all of us perceive and react to situations differently based on how doubt has primed us?

As you experience your day, pay attention to how you react to what goes on outside and inside of you. Try to see which situations lead to unpleasant feelings and which have no effect on you at all.

Try this as an assignment: Record your reactions for the day. See the examples in the table below for a guide, then fill in your own situations and reactions in the table that follows.

SITUATION	REACTION	FEELING
1. Walking outside home and a neighbor's dog is outside.	The dog won't like me. The dog will bite me.	Fear
2. I cannot alter my PowerPoint presentation.	I'll never learn how to make it right. I'll get fired.	Anxious
3. I see a friend at the store, and during a friendly conversation he seems rushed.	The person is annoyed at me for something.	Hurt
4. I am having difficulty assembling the piece of furniture I just purchased.	I can never build these things. It never works for me.	Frustrated, helpless

Now you try.

SITUATION	REACTION	FEELING
1.		

SITUATION	REACTION	FEELING
2.		
3.		

The Situation Is Now Seen Through the Lens of Doubt

Once doubt is activated, you begin to second-guess yourself, and you are bombarded with thoughts. Thoughts driven by doubt are self-critical, fear driven, and typically negative. There is a tendency to stop attending to all the other external and internal stimuli and to hone in on the specific experience(s) that pushed the doubt button. You forget about situational factors and believe you are to blame.

Let's examine the situations from Doubt Test 3 more closely. We'll list some realistic responses that can replace your doubt response.

1. Your colleague walked into the office and did not say hello to you.

DOUBT RESPONSE	REALISTIC RESPONSE
I wonder if he's mad at me.	From past experience the most likely explanation is he's distracted thinking about his personal or professional problems.
Maybe I forgot to do something he asked me to do.	The fact is he did ask me to help him with something, and I am currently working on it. He knows that.

2. Your boss calls to tell you he wants to meet with you later today.

DOUBT RESPONSE	REALISTIC RESPONSE
Maybe he's not happy with me.	The fact is I have gotten positive feedback from him just the other day.
He's going to ask for something unreasonable.	I've got some free time later this afternoon; I can take care of whatever he needs.

3. Your friend cancels lunch with no explanation as to why.

DOUBT RESPONSE	REALISTIC RESPONSE
She doesn't like me very much.	She is a good friend who calls me all the time to get together. What a drag, I guess something came up.
Maybe she had something better to do.	She has family in town and is most likely stuck entertaining them.

4. You don't get invited to a neighbor's holiday party.

DOUBT RESPONSE	REALISTIC RESPONSE
I'm always being snubbed, I should have been invited.	I wish I were invited. Maybe this year they're inviting only relatives.
I did not make the list.	So what, it's one less thing I have to do.

5. You need to call someone for help because she has more expertise in what you're working on.

DOUBT RESPONSE	REALISTIC RESPONSE
She'll be upset that I'm bothering her.	She has encouraged me to ask and always seem genuinely interested in helping me out.
I can't believe I cannot do this myself.	It's smart to use her as a resource.

6. You'll be late on a deadline.

DOUBT RESPONSE	REALISTIC RESPONSE
My boss will be mad.	I'm doing the best I can. It will get done.
I might lose my job.	I can talk to the boss before it's late and maybe we can work something out. It is the nature of this job to run behind.

7. A friend is upset with you.

DOUBT RESPONSE	REALISTIC RESPONSE
He doesn't want to be my friend.	He has gotten upset with me before, and we have always stayed friends.
I messed up again.	We always work it out.

8. A family member is angry at you.

DOUBT RESPONSE	REALISTIC RESPONSE
I'm a bad relative.	I am thoughtful and considerate of my family and their needs. She still loves me.
No matter what I do it's never enough.	This is par for the family course. Just because she wants more doesn't mean I'm not doing enough.

9. You get lost and will be late for a meeting.

DOUBT RESPONSE	REALISTIC RESPONSE
They will think less of me.	They will be concerned that I am lost.
There will be horrible consequences.	I'll give myself ten more minutes and then call them. They'll wait to start this meeting until I get there.

10. The person you are talking to looks at her watch.

DOUBT RESPONSE	REALISTIC RESPONSE
She'd rather be with someone else.	She could be looking at her watch for lots of reasons, not because she doesn't like me or want to be with me.
I must be boring her.	She is always looking at her watch. That's just the way she is.

You can capture your thoughts before doubt biases you into believing negative or fearful interpretations that are not valid. Just because you think it, doesn't mean it's true.

Beware of Negative Emotions

When you view any situation through a negatively biased lens, you experience unpleasant emotions such as fear, sadness, anger, discouragement, hopelessness, and agitation. Many of us are more aware of our emotions than we are of our thoughts. Guess what? You can learn to use your emotions as signals telling you to pay attention to your thoughts. Think about the yellow warning light inside your car. When it goes on, you know that something isn't quite right.

Think about one of your friendships in which your friend relies on you for emotional support and social activities. Was there a time where you had to cancel plans and she blasted you over the phone? Did you notice that her emotional reaction was way out of proportion to the situation? She probably responded with anger or hurt. Perhaps her doubt was activated and took the form of "I don't matter" or "She doesn't care about me anymore" or "I'm being rejected." However, maybe all of her interpretations were incorrect and unnecessarily upsetting. Perhaps the fact was that a meeting was unexpectedly scheduled for that time or a sick child was at home.

Take one of Andrea's situations for example: She's just gotten her three children dressed, fed, and to school. She's on her way to work about to make a right on red. The car in front of her starts to go and then suddenly stops. She rolls into it and damages both cars. Suddenly she is overcome with panic, and the doubt takes over. "I shouldn't be driving." "I'm not a good driver." She imagines the black mark on her driving record. Rather than looking at her overall driving record, she believes every thought in that moment and fears getting back into her car.

A realistic response, one not driven by doubt, would be: "A fender bender would shake anyone up. I've been driving for more than twenty-three years at least five times each day and this is only my second accident. I'd say based on those statistics I'm a competent driver. Feelings aren't facts."

When your negative emotions take over, you thwart yourself. Having lost the confidence to believe in yourself, you cease to reach for your goals; instead you retreat, sabotaging or evading your success.

Doubt-Driven Actions

Take a moment and think about your typical reactions to the obstacle in the road. At home or at work, are you the one to jump in and try to solve the problem or take charge? If your self-doubt arises, you would feel overwhelmed and probably give up without trying. Envision that your child has just told you that a huge project is due tomorrow and you are already swamped with your own paperwork. Do you size up what has to be done and then encourage your child to work independently until help is needed while tackling your own work? Although it's a time crunch and you wish your child had started the project earlier, you recognize it's still possible to get it all done by just digging in. Alternatively, does your doubt lead to panic? Do you think, "It's too late now, it will never get done" and so quit before you start? People feel helpless when they doubt that they can handle something, even if they can.

Does your doubt lead you to typically concede to others, putting their needs above yours? Or do you balance your needs and theirs by choosing a path that accommodates all of you? Suppose you scheduled an appointment for a facial, chiropractor, massage, time at the gym, or coffee with a friend. It really could be any appointment that you were looking forward to. Then an overbearing family member or friend who always takes advantage of you calls and asks for a favor that would entail canceling your appointment. Do you politely let him or her know you are unavailable and then enjoy your day as planned or let the person know you will be free at another time? Or do you let doubt win, giving into your fear of not being a good person or not being liked and say yes when you want to say no?

The action you take in any given situation is driven by how you look at the scenario in question. When you feel down, you see the world through a dark negative lens, and you choose behavioral strategies driven by despair or hopelessness. You isolate, withdraw, or give up. When you feel angry and perceive an injustice, you find yourself responding defensively—with aggression, passivity, or passive aggressiveness. When you feel anxious, you have concluded that you are in danger and unable to handle the circumstances, so the action you take is to avoid or flee the situation. The danger may be social rejection, bodily harm, endless worries, or any number of other concerns. The belief that you cannot handle the situation, or cope, is driven by self-doubt and the discounting of resources within and outside of yourself that you fail to recognize. This perception of danger and the belief that you cannot effectively ward off the danger leads you to avoid or hide from a situation or fight a threat that may not be there.

Depending on the action or inaction you choose and whether you are able to accurately perceive each situation, your doubt is either affirmed or contradicted. Remember the obstacle in the road. If you choose to retreat, sabotage, or evade, your doubt will grow, but if you choose action, your doubt will subside. It is the choice of action—to proceed or not to proceed—that makes the difference.

Making Rules

Doubt leads people to set up all kinds of rules for themselves. These rules govern our actions. They are an internal operating program that helps you organize your world. Over time, doubt can add shortcuts that actually limit our thinking and, consequently, what we're able to do. Usually these assumptions are in the form of *if/then statements*, internal messages from family members or significant others or self-imposed, rigidly held rules.

For example, if I believe that I am not smart enough, I might develop a rule that says I must be perfect all the time. Now with that rule, *if* I make any mistake or *if* there is a disappointment, criticism, malfunction, fiasco, or failure, *then* there is solid proof that I'm not smart enough. A typical rule that develops out of this doubt is the belief that *if* I do everything perfectly, *then* I am smart enough. If it were possible to be perfect all the time, there would be no problem and confidence would prevail. Because perfection is unattainable all the time and rarely definable, doubt is usually the winner.

John's doubt lies with his perception of how likable he is by others. The family message he grew up with was that you're only as popular as the number of friends you have. Another family rule was to keep busy and active playing outside with your friends. When John was a boy, he developed the rule that if he had someone to play with, he was likable and if he was alone with no plans, then he was unlikable. Because it is impossible to always have plans and life is busy, doubt is the winner, and John believes he is unlikable.

You can learn to identify your own rules and rewrite them, reducing the unreasonable demands you place on yourself. Instead of demanding perfection to feel good about yourself, accept that mistakes and shortcomings are what it means to be human. The goal is to make your rules flexible and obtainable.

The Bottom Line

In this chapter you learned to differentiate realistic concern from doubt. Realistic concern is recognizing you are not equipped to successfully deal with a particular situation. Doubt, on the other hand, leads you to unrealistically question your ability to handle the situation, resulting in ineffective action. By understanding your doubt model, you can recognize how doubt gets activated and distorts everything you think, feel, and do.

Chapter Two

Give Doubt a Name

Imagine you have to be hospitalized. Maybe you have to have bypass surgery, your gallbladder removed, or your appendix out. Your friends and relatives surround you and balloons and gifts of food fill your room. How do you feel emotionally? Are you frustrated and discouraged sulking about the activities you are missing or the income you are losing? Are you doing okay and actually enjoying all the love and attention?

Now imagine two weeks have passed and although out of the hospital, you are still recovering from surgery. Friends and family have stopped visiting, and the gifts of food and goodies have stopped. You are more mobile and able to accomplish tasks, run errands, do some work, and take care of things for yourself. Has your mood improved? Are you confident you can take charge of your life again? Or are you feeling blue missing all the company and the kind gifts?

The way you react to this situation tells a lot about whether you place more self-value and importance on your capability or your desirability. Immediately after the surgery, if you despair over your capacity to be productive and independent, you probably tend to value your competence. You want people to think you are smart and capable. Two weeks later, once you are mobile again, your despair lifts; because you are able to be productive, you feel fine. If rather than being frustrated in the hospital you enjoy the attention from your family, then you probably place more value on your relationships and therefore your desirability. You care most about having people in your life or being liked. Two weeks later, the company and phone calls dwindle; your mood sinks because you believe no one cares or you don't matter.

Researchers have identified two main types of personality styles. The first type relies on competence for self-definition, whereas the other type relies on relationships for self-definition. Your individual view of yourself makes you differentially vulnerable to achievement-related or interpersonal events. At the core of doubt is an uncertainty of one's competence or desirability or both.

According to Dr. Aaron T. Beck's theory,* individuals with a competence personality style are independent and action oriented. Accomplishing what they have set out to do is more important than the values or opinions of others. Their self-worth is based on achievement or goals obtained. Therefore, being unable to perform or succeed will lead to doubt.

Individuals with a desirability personality style, according to Beck's theory, derive more self-value from their relationships with others. They are more concerned with being disapproved of and are negatively affected when others disagree, discount, or reject them. Thus a perceived criticism or slight will lead to doubt.

*A. T. Beck, "Cognitive Therapy of Depression: New Perspectives," in *Treatment of Depression: Old Controversies and New Approaches,* ed. P. Clayton and J. Barrett (265–290). New York: Raven, 1983.

We all have doubt labels. In fact, there are an infinite number of them because each one of us has a unique nasty name we call ourselves when our doubt is talking to us. This doubt is connected to what you value most—your competency or your desirability or both. In fact, doubt is more likely to get activated in situations directly related to what you value. For individuals who value competence, doubt is more likely to be activated in achievement-related situations. For individuals who value relationships, doubt is more likely to be activated in social situations. In this chapter, we'll help you learn your personality style and then help you define your specific label of doubt. Knowing the words to define one's doubt is essential. By labeling your doubt, you're better able to see it operating and how it colors your perceptions, inhibits your choices, and fuels your negative, unpleasant feelings.

Competence-Driven Personality

According to Beck, autonomous or competence-driven people's self-worth is based on self-focused judgments regarding achievement-related events. You are goal driven and action oriented. You make work a priority, and base how you feel about yourself on your achievement and success. You are like the salesman who strives for the highest numbers each month or like the athlete whose greatest desire is to win the race. Doubt about your competence is activated under times of criticism, in situations that create a loss of control or loss of independence, and when facing difficulty achieving your goals.

Can You Relate to Sam?
Sam is a competency-oriented person who defines himself by his successes. Sam grew up in the shadow of his arrogant, overbearing,

successful father. Despite Sam's efforts and multiple accomplishments, his father repeatedly let him know that he did not measure up. His father constantly reminded him that he would never be half the man that he was. Sam's mother reinforced this message by always pointing out Sam's shortcomings and never praising his accomplishments. Sam, now fifty-seven years old, is still waiting for his parents' approval.

Sam is the picture of success. He is happily married, financially successful, and talented in many areas. Yet, at the slightest expressed or perceived criticism, doubt is activated, and he crumbles internally. Criticism, in his eyes, means that the other person doubts his talent, his brains, his success—exactly what he doubts in himself.

Desirability-Driven Personality

People who are more concerned with being desirable, good, or worthy fall into the domain of desirability. According to Beck, sociotropic, or what we refer to as desirability-driven, individuals depend on others for their self-worth and need people around them to satisfy their needs, justify their values, and to provide reassurance. Doubt labels can develop from perceived rejection, disappointment, or disagreement with another.

Can You Relate to Jill?
Jill's self-worth centers on her desirability. She defines herself based on her attractiveness to others and is preoccupied with being a good person. Jill grew up in a home with three sisters, all of them blond, blue eyed, and lean. Jill considered herself the ugly duckling with her dark hair, dark eyes, and stockier body type. She always felt she

did not measure up to the rest of the family and believed she was never good enough to be loved. That perception was compounded by what she described as a lack of attention, praise, and love.

Jill's belief that she was unloved led her to conclude that she needed to be perfect to be loved. She thus strived to be the perfect child, always compliant, a good student, and sacrificing her needs and choices for others. However, the strategy backfired. Instead of getting lots of positive attention, she got less attention than the other siblings. Because she was so well behaved, her parents could leave Jill on cruise control while they managed the problems of their other daughters. Instead of being thanked and praised for her generosity and thoughtfulness, she felt taken advantage of and never good enough to be loved.

Jill continues to give and give, rescuing her sisters from their problems and taking the full burden of responsibility in helping her aging parents. Although she is now trim and attractive, one failed relationship after another only serves to confirm to her that she is not good enough to be loved. A delayed phone call, the wandering eye of the man she is with, a cancellation of plans by a friend, or a real or seeming insult leads her to despair. Jill's despair is a result of her perceived rejection and a confirmation of her unattractiveness, inability to measure up, and unlovability.

Determining Your Personality Type

The first step in defining your doubt label is understanding your personality style. Do you have a competency-driven personality or a desirability-driven personality? Perhaps you are driven by both competency and desirability. Take the quizzes in this section to uncover your personality.

DO YOU DERIVE SELF-WORTH FROM COMPETENCY?

Answer true, false, or undecided to the following questions.

1. Nothing feels better than getting a task done.
   True   False   Undecided

2. You gain self-esteem from being paid well for the work you do.
   True   False   Undecided

3. When your personal life conflicts with your professional obligations, you usually make the professional obligation the priority.
   True   False   Undecided

4. You do not compromise everything for your personal life.
   True   False   Undecided

5. Although you appreciate being told that you are loved, you prefer to be considered competent.
   True   False   Undecided

6. When something does not go right, you first think about how you might have messed up.
   True   False   Undecided

7. You would not cancel a revenue-generating task for a social engagement.
   True   False   Undecided

8. You take succeeding in love for granted and work hard to succeed in what you do.
   True   False   Undecided

9. You define yourself by what you do and not by how much you are liked.

   True   False   Undecided

10. You can comfortably do things on your own, including eating out, traveling, and pursuing your interests.

    True   False   Undecided

11. You cannot help being somewhat competitive across situations.

    True   False   Undecided

12. Although you appreciate being told what a good person you are, you prefer to be thought of as smart.

    True   False   Undecided

SELF-ANALYSIS

Add up your true responses: _____

Add up your false responses: _____

Add up your undecided responses: _____

If you have more true responses than false, you base how you feel about yourself on your competency. You define yourself by what you do and you care most about being capable and independent. If you answered more false responses than anything else, then you base how you feel about yourself on your desirability. You are less concerned with what you do and more concerned with being liked and being a good person. If you deliberated on each question and have a lot of undecided responses, then you are the person who is high on both competency and desirability. You care about being competent *and* being liked. You are likely to be under stress because both performance and interpersonal issues are likely to activate your doubt.

DO YOU DERIVE SELF-WORTH FROM DESIRABILITY?

Answer true, false, or undecided to the following questions.

1. The best gift in the world is to be told you are loved.
   True   False   Undecided

2. It is more important to be considered nice than to be seen as smart.
   True   False   Undecided

3. You think about others more often than yourself.
   True   False   Undecided

4. You care about what people think of you and want them to think you are a good person.
   True   False   Undecided

5. Whenever possible you would pick a personal obligation over a professional one when the two are in conflict.
   True   False   Undecided

6. You want everyone to like you.
   True   False   Undecided

7. You recognize you are not as competitive as other people.
   True   False   Undecided

8. You try not to step on anyone's toes.
   True   False   Undecided

9. You do not feel the need to be in charge.
   True   False   Undecided

10. You would prefer to do a social activity rather than your planned goal for the day.
    True   False   Undecided

11. Having your mobility compromised is not the end of the world.
    True   False   Undecided

12. Winning the good citizen award means more than winning first place.
    True   False   Undecided

SELF-ANALYSIS

Add up your true responses: _____

Add up your false responses: _____

Add up your undecided responses: _____

If you have more true responses than false, you have confirmed that you are more desirability driven than competency driven. If you answered mostly false to these questions, your competency or need to succeed was confirmed. Were you caught once again in the middle, teetering between true and false? Then you are indeed driven by both competency and desirability. Keep your answers in mind when you look for the labels of your doubt.

The Connection Between Who We Are and Doubt

Each of us has a label for the doubt we carry inside of us. This label reflects the personality style that more strongly reflects your self-definition, as you determined by taking the last two quizzes. However, if you answered undecided to many of the questions in both quizzes, then you will need to look for doubt labels in both categories. Now

that you have defined your personality style, you can put a label on
your doubt.

Competence Doubt

Let's start with the competency personality style. Remember you
are the person who wants to win the race, be seen at the top of
what you do, or acknowledged for your brains or talents. Because
you care so much about succeeding, you are more vulnerable at
doubting yourself in this area. Your doubt surfaces when faced
with obstacles in your path to success. We call this category of
doubt *competence doubt*.

Sit quietly for a moment and think about the names you call
yourself when you are experiencing doubt: "I'm _____." What is the
doubt label you have for yourself? If you are having trouble, think
about last time you got really upset or anxious or frustrated. It probably had something to do with work, school, sports, responsibility, or
a goal. Imagine yourself back in that situation. As you start to notice
your distress increase, try to remember the "I statement" that was
going through your mind. If your self-doubt is competency, here are
some examples of things you may have said to yourself: "I'm stupid,"
"I'm not good enough," "I'm weak," "I'm inadequate," "I'm a failure."

Let's Take a Look Back at Sam

Sam is helping his son make an erupting volcano for his third-
grade science project. Sam has spent countless hours online
researching how to do this and many hours walking through craft
stores to find the exact ingredients to make the best eruption with
lava flow. He tries not to get short with his son while working on
the project each time his son asks if they're done already or when
the boy carelessly places plastic figures around the volcano. Sam
also tries not to make it too nearly perfect for fear that the science

teacher will know that he took over the project. On the day the project is due, Sam insists on driving his son to school so that the project does not get bumped on the bus; he then eagerly waits for the teacher's report. That evening, his son tells Sam he got a B+ on the project. Sam becomes distressed and starts to barrage his son with questions wanting to know the teacher's specific comments as well as how many other grades were better. Sam's thoughts are filled with could-haves and should-haves, and he has images of his dad saying, "I could have done it better, you loser." Sam's doubt gets the best of him, and he thinks, "I can't do anything right and it's never good enough." Sam's doubt label of "I'm incompetent" led him to view his son's grade as proof of his own inadequacy.

Desirability Doubt

Let's look at the typical doubt of the desirability personality. Remember you are the person who cares about being liked and/ or being a good person. You constantly seek the approval of others and need others to validate you. The content of your doubt is about being desirable or liked.

Sit back for a moment and think about the names you call yourself during or right after an upsetting situation: "I'm _____." The names stemming from doubt are typically based on an interpersonal theme. Here are some examples of your doubt label: "I'm unlikable," "I'm unattractive," "I'm a bad [mother, sister, father, brother, friend, spouse]," "I'm boring." When you look for the meaning behind your actions or another person's actions, you conclude something derogatory about your desirability.

Let's Take a Look Back at Jill

Jill is getting ready for her sister's wedding. One sister is already married, and the other sister will be bringing her significant other.

Jill's boyfriend broke up with her a month ago. As she walks down the aisle, Jill feels the stares from the audience and has images of people pointing her out as the only single one or calling her an "old maid." At the reception, people seem to feel the need to tell her that she will find eventually someone. All Jill can think is, "Everyone has someone to love but me." "My last boyfriend broke it off because he said I was not right for him." "I'm not right for anyone." Jill's doubt label is "I'm unlovable."

Another Way to Uncover the Doubt Label

If you're still having difficulty identifying your doubt label or if you want an additional exercise to confirm that label, consider the following. Think of a situation in which you perceive an injustice has or had been done to you. Here's an example: Someone owes you money and has not paid you back. You don't think you have the courage to ask for the money. Now ask yourself, What does it mean that you don't have the courage? Does it mean you are weak, powerless, or gutless? Or does it mean that you are not particularly concerned because the person probably just forgot? Perhaps not asking for the money doesn't make you weak, powerless, or gutless; it may not mean anything about you at all. The meaning we ascribe to our own and other people's behavior is linked to our doubt label. What does it mean to you that this injustice or wrongdoing took place? What conclusions do you have for why the person hasn't volunteered to pay you back? Are you driven by competency doubt?

If instead of doubting your competency, you doubt your desirability, you'll perceive the situation differently. You may feel that the friend did not pay back the money because he doesn't care about you. Your overall conclusion could then be that he doesn't care about you because basically you are undesirable, unlovable, unlikable, or flawed. If you do not doubt your desirability, you would draw no such conclusions from your friend's behavior. You recognize you are desirable, lovable, likable, or not flawed regardless of whether he pays you back or not.

To uncover the label of your own doubt:

1. Identify the perceived injustice or wrong: Look for a should statement about yourself or others, and you will have an easier time identifying the injustice. Did you think someone else or yourself should have done something that she or you did not? Did you think someone else or yourself should not have done something she or you did? Identifying the *broken should rule* will lead you to your perceived injustice.

2. Ask yourself what it means about you that the other person did not do what you expected.

3. Ask yourself what it means about you that you did what you did in response to the other person's action or inaction.

4. Identify your doubt label: This is the meaning you give to what transpired.

You may find one word here that is just right for your doubt or perhaps it will take several words to describe that doubt. The doubt label is what you say when you are self-critical or beating yourself up. Do not be surprised if your label of doubt is not listed in this book because there are infinite labels, and they are personally developed.

Let's look at a few examples of determining a doubt label.

Bill, a wealthy businessman, dropped out of college to support his family after his father got sick. At age sixty-three, he spends most of his time working and on the weekend is often bored when he is unable to go into the office. His wife, an avid reader, suggests he read, too. This provides support for Bill's doubt label of "I am stupid." Here's how you can uncover Bill's doubt label.

1. **Perceived wrong:** "My wife thinks I should be reading, and I should read."

2. **Meaning:** "My wife thinks I am inferior because I don't read."

3. **Meaning:** "I must not be smart or intellectual, or I would read."

4. **Label:** "I am stupid."

Look at another situation. Kate called her husband at work only to find that he was preoccupied and did not seem to be paying attention to anything she was saying. He then said that he needed to go and would call her later. This provides her with evidence that her doubt label "I am unwanted" is true. Here's how you can uncover Kate's doubt label.

1. **Perceived wrong:** "He should want to talk to me."

2. **Meaning:** "My husband is not interested in what I have to say."

3. **Meaning:** "He doesn't care about me."

4. **Label:** "I am unwanted."

Did you identify with both Sam and Kate? If you care about

being both competent and desirable, you related to the competency doubt that was activated in Bill and the desirability doubt in Kate. Therefore, these examples together would trigger this doubt label: "I am stupid and unwanted."

Joe exemplifies the person who has doubt in both areas. Joe gets called into his boss's office for his yearly evaluation. His boss says, "Let's starts with the strengths and then we'll move on to the weaknesses, which is standard procedure." Joe barely hears the strengths because his mind is racing to all of the possible weaknesses. He keeps thinking, "I always try my best, stay late, and meet the company's goals. I also get along with everyone, help anyone who needs it, and go the extra mile for my boss." In addition, he begins to think that maybe his work quality is an issue and that he has disappointed his boss who obviously no longer likes him. Joe sees only the information that supports his doubt label of "I am not good enough professionally or interpersonally." Here's how you can discover Joe's doubt label.

1. **Perceived wrong:** "There should not be any weakness because of all I have done."

2. **Meaning:** "My boss thinks I'm not cutting it, and I've disappointed him."

3. **Meaning:** "I've let him down in my work and as his employee."

4. **Label:** "I'm not good enough professionally or interpersonally."

People who highly value both competency and desirability are more likely to identify doubt labels in both domains. Your doubt label does not have to be these specific words. The labels come from whatever nasty name(s) you call yourself. Perhaps you will find your own labels in the following list.

Doubt Label Examples

COMPETENCY DOUBT LABEL	DESIRABILITY DOUBT LABEL
I'm stupid.	I'm unlikable.
I'm not good enough to succeed.	I'm not good enough to be loved.
I'm weak.	I'm inferior.
I'm inadequate.	I'm unattractive.
I'm a failure.	I'm bad.
I'm incompetent.	I'm undesirable.
I'm a fraud.	I'm unwanted.

Where Did Your Doubt Label Come From?

We are sociobiological creatures. All of us have a genetic makeup that shapes our temperament. Did you ever wonder why some babies waken at the slightest noise, whereas others sleep peacefully with chaos around them? As those same babies age, you might notice that some are easily rattled, but others are very calm. The social world, including our life experiences, the messages we hear, and the interactions with others all affect our biological temperaments helping make us the people we become.

Which life experiences matter and which ones do not are different for every individual. Children of great adversity can crumble or demonstrate great psychological strength and remain unscathed by their traumas. Children of secure and safe upbringings may be psychologically compromised or may stand confident. Clearly, some childhood experiences are more likely to result in compromised self-worth and confidence. People who have experienced abuse, neglect,

Additional Strategies to Use to Uncover Your Doubt Label

There are many ways to uncover your doubt label. Here is a list of some strategies you may want to try.

1. Think about the last upsetting situation you experienced.

2. Think about your worst experience.

3. Think about what you worry about.

4. Think about what stresses you out.

5. Mentally tick through your day. What do you bypass and what do you focus on?

6. Image an ideal day. What wouldn't go wrong?

7. How do you respond to mistakes?

8. How do you respond to criticism?

As you answered these questions, what kinds of situations distressed you the most? Were they performance related? Did they impede your independence? If so, look for labels of doubt about competence or powerlessness. Were they related to social situations? If so, look for labels of undesirability. Were they related to both performance and social situations? If so, look for labels of doubt in both domains. To further uncover your label of doubt, consider what it means about you that what happened took place or that you responded the way you did. Identifying your doubt label will make it easier to eliminate it!

or trauma understandably often have a more negative self-view. But, the derogatory label you have come to call yourself is unique, even if someone else has experienced the same type of abuse.

What other life experiences shape doubt? Here is a list of situations that people report as playing a significant role in the way they have come to view themselves.

- Parents getting divorced.

- Conflict in the household.

- Chronic illness or death of a family member or significant other.

- Relocating to a new area.

- Not being picked for a team on the playground or in school.

- Not making the traveling or varsity sports team the first time they tried out.

- Sitting in the last chair in orchestra.

- Needing reading enrichment in the first grade.

- Always the first one out in a spelling bee.

- Struggling with math homework.

- Not being good at sports at a young age.

- Not being interested in sports at a young age.

- Not getting a part in the play or the chorus.

- Being bullied or ridiculed.

- Not being invited to a birthday party or included in social plans.

Doubt Can Change over Time

The major domain of our doubt tends to become fixed over time. But how strongly we derive our self-worth from our competency or desirability moves along a continuum throughout our life and thus affects the overall picture of doubt. Certain developmental milestones more strongly pull us in one direction or the other on the continuum.

As students and new professionals, most of us are trying to succeed and therefore tend to place more value on performance-related goals. It is during these times that doubt about our competence may get activated to some degree. However, the person with a competency doubt label will yell louder about the work rather than the relationships.

During the stage of life when we may be more invested in pursuing a significant other or when the desire to have a child increases, social goals tend to become more of a priority. Doubt about being loved and accepted may get more activated during this time. However, the individual with a desirability doubt label is more likely to suffer during this process.

As we age, we may be pulled from one end of the continuum to the other or closer to the middle. Regardless of where we fall on the personality domain, self-doubt will still speak to us if we let it.

You can see how any one of these events may seem insignificant in the broader picture of one's life, but in a vulnerable psyche just one of these could provide the fertilizer for doubt to grow. The impact of the event is affected by how we interpret what happened. Take the example of the playground. Two captains have nominated themselves, and they are picking teams for football, tag, or kickball. The teams are picked, and you are not on a team. What do you think? The child who has already begun to doubt her competence may think, "I stink, no wonder they did not pick me." "I'm never good enough." "I'm a failure." The child who has already begun to doubt her desirability may think, "I thought they were my friends, how could they not pick me, they must not like me after all. I'm unlikable."

Seemingly unimportant events start to accumulate into a convincing case to reinforce self-doubt. Think about the label of doubt you have uncovered in yourself. See if you can now think back to your past and identify events that contributed to this doubt. Maybe you can remember things from your early childhood, your teenage years, your young adulthood, or even events in your current life that all seem to support your doubt. To remove doubt, it is essential to understand where it came from. Just because the doubt made sense to us based on our life situations does not make the doubt valid.

Strengthening Our Doubt Label

Once doubt has negatively colored our self-view, it seeks information to confirm itself. Remember Sam, the successful businessman who thinks he does not measure up? Sam has spent his entire life living in his father's shadow.

By never getting recognition for his accomplishments he came to believe he did not measure up and no one was truly his ally or supporter. Mom reinforced his doubt by telling him, "Without me you would be garbage" and by always asking him to deliver more while telling him he never delivered enough. Sam's father was also emotionally abusive, battering him verbally.

Sam is not only waiting for the validation of his parents but searches for it in all spheres of his life. Understandably, when his parents failed to acknowledge his fiftieth birthday and continued to ignore his financial and personal success, his belief that he does not measure up gets perpetuated. When they question the amount of money he spends on entertainment, he believes his competency is under scrutiny. Outside of his immediate family, he often interprets situations as evidence of others' letting him down, not supporting him and questioning his competency. For example, when a friend or relative does not take his side in a dispute, it means he is not his ally and that he is questioning his judgment and competence. This once again confirms his belief that he does not measure up. Even minor debates activate Sam's doubt if his view is not supported, such as what time or where to eat lunch, how much tip to leave, or whether to let a person join the golf group after someone has already teed off.

Remember Jill? She is the only unattached sister. She grew up believing she never measured up to the rest of the family and that she was not good enough to be loved. Jill began to doubt her desirability at a young age. Because she always thought she was never good enough to be truly loved, she saw all of her life experiences through that lens. When her sisters were complimented, she always assumed she fell short and knew she was undeserving of such compliments. When her friends were showered with hugs and kisses, she thought, "How come no one loves me like that?" As she matured, she believed her sisters were adored by their boyfriends and later by their husbands while she remained single and alone; thus, she believed she was unloved. When people at work took advantage of her or looked out for themselves with no consideration for her, she believed it was because they did not like her. When one relationship after another did not work out, she assumed it was because she was never good enough to make others love her.

The Bottom Line

In this chapter you have learned a lot about yourself. You have gained an understanding of your personality, and you now know whether you are more competency driven, desirability driven, or both competency and desirability driven. You have become skilled at identifying the label of doubt. You have gained knowledge about where your doubt came from and understand how it has grown and gathered strength.

Step 2
Question It

Chapter Three

Check Out Your Doubt

In this chapter, we will teach you to map out doubt so you view the whole picture. As you discovered in Step 1, feelings, behaviors, body reactions, and even motivation can be colored by the lens of doubt. The question is, How accurate are your perceptions? We also will teach you how to identify when doubt is talking and examine the extent to which it is true or not true and if it is realistic or unwarranted. It's time to put that logical part of your brain back in the driver's seat and stop accepting doubt as irrefutable evidence.

Listening to Our Thoughts

Most of us never think to stop and say, "What's going through my mind?" as we notice a shift in our mood or a change in our body. Rather than our thoughts, we tend to be more aware of changes in body or mood. The shift in our mood can be suddenly feeling down, anxious, fearful, mad, or even frustrated. Changes in our body can be increased heart rate, sweating, headache, restlessness, muscle tension, backache, or nausea, just to name a few. However, it is the thoughts tied to your feelings or discomfort in your body that let you know you have been *doubt activated*. That is why it is so important to pay attention to your internal voice and to examine the credibility of the actual message. Building your examination skills and realistically understanding your risk in comparison to your internal and external assets will help put you back in control of your life so you can unblock the paths to success.

How do you begin to examine your doubt? The Doubt Register is used to record situations and examine the accuracy of doubt. It also helps you distinguish between realistic concern and global doubt. The Doubt Register is one of the most important tools for squashing doubt. How does it work?

It's as easy as learning the ABCs!

A is for the **activating situation**.

B is for the **body response**.

C is for **cognitions** (your perceptions and interpretations).

D is for **doubt**.

E is for **emotion**.

F is for the **facts** of the situation (which you'll collect and logically examine).

G is for **go time: rethink, relax, and respond**.

The Doubt Register helps you deconstruct doubt. First, you identify the specific activating situation (**A**) including both internal and external situations. Next, you record what your body (**B**) is experiencing, or your physical sensations. Your perceptions of the activating situations are then recorded as cognitions (**C**). Then your doubt (**D**) label is identified and recorded. After that, you make note of your emotions (**E**). Next, you examine the accuracy of your thoughts and doubt through specific questions that lead you to see the facts (**F**). Situational and global doubt is differentiated. Last, it's go time (**G**), when you learn to rethink the situation, relax the intensity of the body response or emotion, and respond effectively to your doubt.

Let's examine each of these steps in more detail, so you can learn how to use the Doubt Register on your own. Throughout this chapter, you'll find sample Doubt Registers as well as blank registers to fill in for yourself. You'll also find a blank Doubt Register at the end of the book, to fill in as you wish. It is important to use the Doubt Register so thoughts don't get twisted and turned in your head to fit doubt. Writing on paper allows you to examine your doubt in a logical and rational way.

A: Activating Situation

Any given situation can affect each of us in a different way. It is not the situation itself that activates doubt but rather the interpretation of it. For individuals with competency doubt, these are usually circumstances in which they are frustrated by the belief that their performance will be negatively received, which activates doubt. For individuals with desirability doubt, activating situations are interpersonal events that did not go the way they imagined.

Can You Relate to Sam?
Sam is playing pool with several friends and one of them recommends that he use a different shot. His friend also suggests that

Sam should use a bridge rather than stretching himself to go for the bank shot. In another situation, Sam is at his weekly poker game, and his neighbor whispers in his ear exactly how he should play the hand. Sam explodes in rage, thinking, "Who are you to give me advice?" Sam feels wounded because he interprets these comments as criticisms about his competency.

Sam's activating situations are recorded on the Doubt Register below.

ACTIVATING SITUATION (SAM)	B	C	D	E	F	G
Playing pool, and a friend suggests how he play the shot.						

ACTIVATING SITUATION (SAM)	B	C	D	E	F	G
Playing poker, and a friend suggests how he play the hand.						

Can You Relate to Jill?

Jill is out to dinner with her family and a friend stops by the table to say hello. The friend tells Jill that she looks like her grandmother, who Jill thinks is a shriveled up, moderately overweight, homely looking woman. On another night, Jill is expecting a man to call; she sits by the phone waiting until he calls two hours after the designated time. Jill takes the comment about her looks and the gentleman's tardiness as rejection and feedback about her unattractiveness and undesirability. Her self-doubt leads her to see these incidents as criticism.

Jill's activating situations are written on the Doubt Register below.

ACTIVATING SITUATION (JILL)	B	C	D	E	F	G
A friend tells Jill she looks like her grandmother.						

ACTIVATING SITUATION (JILL)	B	C	D	E	F	G
A man calls her two hours late.						

Your Turn

After reviewing Sam's and Jill's situations, it's your turn to try using the Doubt Register. Remember a situation can be either internal (what is going on in your own head or body) or external (what is going on outside of you). What activates your doubt? Here are some strategies to help you define a situation that you can use in the Doubt Register:

- Think of the worst situation you have been in lately.

- Pinpoint one or more specific aspects of the situation that upset you rather than summarizing the entire situation as a whole.

- It can be an event or daydream or nightmare or image.

- Try to determine the specific moment when you noticed a shift in your body or emotion or behavior.

- It can be a bodily sensation or a feeling.

- Image a situation and try to figure out when the upset would begin.

Let's use the last event that upset you in some way. Record that event in the Doubt Register:

ACTIVATING SITUATION (YOU)	B	C	D	E	F	G

B: Body Response

Your body supplies you with important clues about how you are perceiving situations and to what extent you are doubt activated. From an evolutionary standpoint, you need to be ready to respond in order to survive. Your sympathetic nervous system prepares your body for action. It operates without conscious thought and becomes more active during times of stress. Sympathetic body responses can include increased heart rate, sweating, restlessness, shakiness, muscle tension, and shortness of breath. Opposite to your sympathetic nervous system is your parasympathetic nervous system, which calms your body down. Body responses can include resting and digesting.

In your own life, think about the last situation in which you felt at risk or vulnerable. It could be realizing that your four-year-old daughter is no longer in the aisle with you in the supermarket. It could be someone swerving into your lane while you are driving. Or it could be forgetting to complete an important task at work or failing to return an important phone call and it's already the end of the day. It is what you feel when you are several hours into a long road trip and you're suddenly jolted out of your conversation because you think you left the stove on. What was going on in your body? We all have different vulnerabilities in our body; you may have experienced a headache, neck or shoulder tension, nausea, diarrhea, dry mouth, or shortness of breath. These body reactions are your clues in later situations that it's time to pay attention to your thoughts so that you know whether you have been doubt activated.

Can You Relate to Sam?

When Sam is facing situations in which friends offer him unsolicited advice, his body tenses up, his heart pounds, and his face flushes.

Sam's body responses are listed on the Doubt Register below.

ACTIVATING SITUATION (SAM)	BODY RESPONSE	C	D	E	F	G
Playing pool, and a friend suggests how he play the shot.	Body tenses up, heart pounds, face flushes.					
Playing poker, and a friend suggests how he play the hand.	Body tenses up, heart pounds, face flushes.					

Can You Relate to Jill?

Regularly, when Jill perceives any form of criticism she experiences overwhelming fatigue; her shoulders slump; and she notices pain in her jaw, head, and neck. When Jill perceives rejection, such as an unreturned call, she becomes aware of exhaustion, jaw clenching, and stomach upset.

Jill's body responses are documented on the Doubt Register on the next page.

ACTIVATING SITUATION (JILL)	BODY RESPONSE	C	D	E	F	G
A friend tells Jill she looks like her grandmother.	Overwhelming fatigue; shoulders slump; pain in jaw, head, and neck.					
A man calls her two hours late.	Exhaustion, jaw clenching, stomach upset.					

Tip *Use your main body symptom as a warning light that it is time to examine your thoughts and doubt.*

Your Turn

Now it's your turn to try using the Doubt Register. Write out each individual, significant body reaction you had in response to the specific activating event that you wrote in the first column. Notice the intensity of the body symptoms and record all of them, regardless of their intensity.

ACTIVATING SITUATION (YOU)	BODY RESPONSE	C	D	E	F	G

C: Cognitions

Do you ever stop and ask yourself what is going through your mind? Most of us never think to do so, do not pay attention, or simply buy into whatever our brain is saying. We are here to tell you not only to *stop* and *think* but to *examine*. Do you automatically buy into whatever someone else is telling you? Of course not! Well, don't do it with yourself.

When you were growing up you weren't offered any courses on thinking. As you think back to your childhood dinner table discussions, do you remember your parents asking you about your day? How did you respond? Did you give them a one-word answer, like "Fine" or "Okay" or "Bad"? Could you label whatever emotion you were feeling? Even more specifically, could you identify the situations or images in your head that were responsible for that feeling? Could you put your finger on the specific thought that began it all?

According to the cognitive model, how we think influences our feelings and our responses. All of us have hundreds of thoughts going through our minds throughout the day, and typically we walk around completely unaware of their effect on us. Think about a discussion you had with a friend or colleague in which you had a completely different understanding of an event. Or picture a situation in which you are in a large group and someone asks you an opinion on something. You pause for a moment and try to put together a response in your head. As you do, you may notice lots of thoughts: "I hope this is what they are looking for"; "I'll sound stupid"; "I don't want to hurt their feelings"; "I'm not prepared." You may notice your face feeling flushed or your hands getting clammy or shakiness in your voice. You deliver your response and observe lots of self-criticisms bogging you down throughout the rest of your day. Later, you talk to your associate. You ask, "So how did I do?" The response is "Nice job" or "I don't remember what you said." Were all those knocks you gave yourself justified? Did you suffer without cause? The thoughts that run through your head are your own situation-specific perceptions of the world around you. When doubt is activated, these perceptions are the direct reflections of that doubt.

Can You Relate to Sam?

Sam is on his way to a board meeting when he realizes that he left several necessary documents sitting on his desk. His doubt response is, "I can't even get the simple things right." "They'll think I'm incompetent." A more realistic response is, "No big deal. I'll have someone in my office fax or run them over; worst-case scenario is I'll turn around and be fifteen minutes late for the meeting."

See Sam's cognitions recorded on the Doubt Register below.

ACTIVATING SITUATION (SAM)	BODY RESPONSE	COGNITIONS	D	E	F	G
Left documents behind.	Heart begins to beat rapidly, starts to sweat.	I can't get even the simple things right. They think I'm incompetent.				

Can You Relate to Jill?

Jill is by the water cooler, and she overhears two friends making lunch plans. Her automatic doubt response is, "They probably won't invite me. They don't really like me." A more realistic response is, "They may invite me if I walk up and strike up a conversation with them" or "I have had lunch with them in the past, so even if I don't get invited today there is no reason to think I won't have lunch plans with them in the future."

Jill's cognitions are recorded on the Doubt Register on the next page.

ACTIVATING SITUATION (JILL)	BODY RESPONSE	COGNITIONS	D	E	F	G
Hears two friends making lunch plans.	Tearful, head-ache, tension.	They probably won't invite me. They don't really like me.				

Your Turn

Now it's your turn to use the Doubt Register. Ask yourself, "What was going through my mind at the specific moment when I noticed distress?" Separate the superficial or descriptor thoughts from the automatic thoughts. *Descriptor thoughts* describe the situation and simply give details of the activating event. Use the Cognitions column of the Doubt Register to identify the perceptions you had of what was going on inside or outside of you. Your perception may not be a thought; you may have an image instead. You can record either in the Cognitions column. The key question is, "What am I thinking?" In the cognition column of the Doubt Register, list the specific thoughts and/or images you had. For guidance, see what Sam and Jill recorded above.

ACTIVATING SITUATION (YOU)	BODY RESPONSE	COGNITIONS	D	E	F	G

Try an experiment: Start asking friends and colleagues their thoughts about various experiences they shared with you throughout the day. When they tell you they spent a lot of money on something or did not invite someone to an event, ask them what thoughts ran through their mind as they told you this. Notice if their thoughts are similar or different from yours. What conclusions can you draw?

D: Doubt

It is impossible to attend to everything going on around you all at one time. For this reason, you have to somehow organize how and to what you pay attention. Take this moment and try to attend to as many things going on around and within you as you can. Where are you? What do you hear? What do you see? How many conversations are going on at once? Is there anybody walking by? Is there background noise—for example, the television or a cell phone conversation? That doesn't even include what you smell, taste, or touch. Add to that all of your internal body sensations and then combine that with more random thoughts like what you'll eat for lunch because your stomach is growling or what time you have to meet someone or whether you remembered to pay a certain bill.

When you are doubt activated, your world is suddenly seen through that lens. You begin to filter your experiences to fit your doubt. The good stuff tends to get ignored or disqualified and the ambiguous, neutral, and negative information gets used to lend credence to doubt. This leaves you filled with lots of skewed doubt-driven thoughts to build and cement your doubt label.

Remember from Chapter 1 that doubt is different from realistic concern. Now, you'll learn to recognize when doubt is activated and learn to question its validity. For instance, you are getting behind the wheel of a car after having taken only a few hours of driving lessons. You are not sure you are ready. After all, you are learning. Realistic concern is appropriate in this situation. However, if you have fears about your ability to drive even after years of experience behind the wheel, that is different. That is global doubt whereby negative emotions arise from unfounded insecurity. Apprehension is unjustifiable in this situation. You can defeat this needless doubt, and we will show you how.

Is Doubt Justified?

Consider the following situations:

The situation: You are scheduled to present a status report at a meeting tomorrow at work. Doubt is activated, is it justified or not?

1. You are behind in your work, and as a result your report is incomplete. (Doubt is justified.)

2. You report is ready, and you know your material well. (Doubt is not justified.)

The situation: You are about to go on a blind date. Doubt is activated, is it justified or not?

1. You have had one uncomfortable cryptic phone exchange with this person, and scheduling the meeting has been a giant hassle. (Doubt is justified.)

2. A good friend arranged the meeting, and you already know the two of you have a lot in common. (Doubt is not justified.)

Realistic Concern

There are definitely times in your life when realistic concern makes sense. You may notice your gut instinct kicking in or your thoughts acting like the warning light in your car. In those instances, there is a definite situation in which you need to prepare for or respond to. Realistic concern can come from having to decide about a medical procedure, resolving a disagreement, or making a career or life decision that will ultimately affect your family. If you have children, think about how many concerns you are faced with at every turn. The key is when you are unprepared or uninformed, realistic concern is warranted and serves as an important guide for handling the situation.

Doubt

Global doubt is not based on the actual events of the situation but rather by doubt activation. What this means is that the way you perceive situations is colored by the lens of doubt, which negatively biases the way you see your world. This fuels your negative emotions, such as fear or worry or distress. As you learned in the last chapter, individuals tend to be differentially vulnerable to achievement-related situations or social situations. However, some people are vulnerable to both. Naming your doubt and knowing when you are more likely to get your buttons pushed are the first steps to regaining control and confidence in your life.

Global doubt can also get activated when you place a lot of meaning on the situation or if something that you value did not go as you imagined or planned. Think about the characteristics from which you derive self-value. For example, is it your intelligence, social finesse, competence, athleticism, compassion, independence, or homemaking? Perhaps you derive self-value from a role. Some of these roles are mother, father, sister, brother, boss, employee, colleague, athlete, brainiac, and friend. Which of your characteristics do you value the most? These are areas in which you are most vulnerable to doubt.

How Stress Plays a Role

Stress can make us more vulnerable to doubt. Stress can be something big or a series of smaller upsets. When you wake up in the morning, stress can be anything that you are confronted with, from your dog peeing on the rug to your child taking a marker to the wall to remembering an assignment at the last minute to an as-you-walk-out-the-door disagreement. Now think about possible bigger issues: the break up of a relationship, birth of a child, health problems, job security, financial distress, impossible deadlines, parent care, and trying to juggle several tasks at the same time. The possibilities of what could be viewed as stressful are staggering. However, the key is to remember that the mental or physical strain comes from your perceptions of the activating situation.

Transition times affect our stress levels, which can in turn activate our self-doubt. There are several factors at play:

- We get used to old roles and struggle with new or expanded ones.

- The older we get, the more responsibilities we tend to have, and so any additional responsibility may become overwhelming.

- Our responsibilities change over time, and we have to either roll with it or stress.

- Our own physical and mental capabilities change and even begin to diminish over time.

Although transition times can increase our stress levels, they don't have to activate our doubt. Confidence comes from experiencing situations without the negative lens of doubt so that we can continue to find meaning and to learn, updating and expanding how we define ourselves.

> **Remember:** *Stress makes us more vulnerable to doubt because it lowers our defenses and weakens our walls of protection, thus creating more opportunities for doubt to express itself. View it as a challenge not as a defeat. Accept that there is no avoiding it.*

Can You Relate to Sam?

Sam is someone who regardless of how prepared he is, thinks he is never prepared enough. Even with a written report and hours of due diligence, he wonders if someone will ask a question to trip him up. Thus, he faces all meetings burdened with the unjustified doubt that he is not good enough.

Always thinking he is not good enough Sam believes he is incompetent. Sam's doubt label I'm incompetent is recorded in the Doubt Register below.

ACTIVATING SITUATION (SAM)	BODY RESPONSE	COGNITIONS	DOUBT LABEL	E	F	G
Left documents behind.	Heart begins to beat rapidly, starts to sweat.	I can't get even the simple things right. They think I'm incompetent.	I'm incompetent.			

Can You Relate to Jill?

Jill dreads her blind date. Despite the facts that her friend has arranged the meeting and she has had numerous amusing phone calls with this man, Jill worries he will find her unattractive and unappealing.

Regardless of positive feedback, self-doubt that she is unlovable always erupts. Jill's doubt label I'm unlovable is shown in the Doubt Register below.

ACTIVATING SITUATION (JILL)	BODY RESPONSE	COGNITIONS	DOUBT LABEL	E	F	G
Hears two friends making lunch plans.	Tearful, head-ache, tension.	They probably won't invite me. They don't really like me.	I'm unlovable.			

Your Turn

After you review Sam's and Jill's entries above in the Doubt Register, it's your turn to record your doubt label. Can you distinguish doubt from realistic concern? Regardless, the culprit behind your distress is doubt. If it is realistic concern, the global doubt label is making the situational doubt worse. Name the doubt label, and record it in the Doubt Register.

ACTIVATING SITUATION (YOU)	BODY RESPONSE	COGNITIONS	DOUBT LABEL	E	F	G

E: Emotion

Emotions, when used correctly, alert us that we need to be paying closer attention to how we are interpreting the activating situation. Emotions can act as a guide when we are not sure about our thoughts or when we have doubt regarding any situation. The first step is to try to label the emotion. Naming your emotion may be more difficult than your think because most of us were not taught to ask ourselves how we feel in response to different events that occur on a daily basis. A good exercise for you may be to begin to ask yourself to label your mood at various points throughout the day. First, see if you can name the emotion, and then pay attention to its strength. Is the emotion barely there, extreme, or somewhere in between? Recognizing when emotions are intense helps us look at our thinking. Learn to label your emotions so you know what you are dealing with. Although the following list is not comprehensive, it will give you a good place to start as you label your emotions:

Sad	Angry	Frustrated
Anxious	Embarrassed	Ashamed
Panicked	Rejected	Happy
Fearful	Lonely	Surprised
Distressed	Guilty	Excited
Irritable	Hurt	Relieved
Frustrated	Afraid	Loving
Agitated	Disgusted	Secure
Hopeless	Insecure	Confident

Ask yourself, What emotion am I feeling? Then ask yourself, Is my emotion whispering at me or screaming?

Chill Those Emotions

When your emotions are screaming, there are tons of strategies you can use to dampen down the intensity. We can all benefit by letting air out of our overfilled tires. When emotions are biasing your perspective and leading you to subjectively based, unreliable conclusions instead of the truth based on factual conclusions, a "timed" time-out will allow you time to calm down and think more clearly. Have you ever been so angry at someone or something that you saw red? Did this cause you to react in a way that you felt badly about once you calmed down? When we say timed time-out we mean taking ten to thirty minutes to allow the intensity of the emotion to drop to below a 7 on a scale of 1 to 10. Then you can think through the situation in a calmer and more rational way because your emotions are no longer coloring or impairing your thoughts.

Consider the following strategies for calming your emotions: Take a walk, exercise, jump up and down, prepare your favorite beverage, bake, cook, barbecue, leaf through a magazine, read your email, call a friend, complete a task, hug or kiss someone, play with your child, cuddle with your pet, run an errand, sit on a bench at a park, look through a photo album, take a shower, take a steam bath, relax in the tub, pat cold water on your face, imagine being in your favorite place or favorite moment, have a conversation, plan a fun activity, list your accomplishments, list all the people you care about, review positive feedback, read the comics, pick up a book, glance through the newspaper, or just laugh.

Can You Relate to Sam?

Sam's long term belief that he is incompetent leads him to doubt himself when he leaves the documents behind. He thinks "I can't get even the simple things right." "They think I'm incompetent." As a result, he feels angry, hurt, and fearful. His emotions are recorded on the Doubt Register on the next page.

Can You Relate to Jill?

Jill's belief that she is unlovable colors her perception when she hears two friends making lunch plans. She thinks "They probably won't invite me." "They don't really like me." This leads her to feel sad and hopeless. Her emotions are recorded on the Doubt Register on the next page.

Your Turn

Review Sam's and Jill's emotions, which they wrote in their Doubt Registers on the next page. Now it's your turn.

ACTIVATING SITUATION (SAM)	BODY RESPONSE	COGNITIONS	DOUBT LABEL	EMOTION	F	G
Left documents behind.	Heart begins to beat rapidly, starts to sweat.	I can't get even the simple things right. They think I'm incompetent.	I'm incompetent.	Anger, hurt, fear.		

ACTIVATING SITUATION (JILL)	BODY RESPONSE	COGNITIONS	DOUBT LABEL	EMOTION	F	G
Hears two friends making lunch plans.	Tearful, headache, tension.	They probably won't invite me. They don't really like me.	I'm unlovable.	Sad, hopeless.		

ACTIVATING SITUATION (YOU)	BODY RESPONSE	COGNITIONS	DOUBT LABEL	EMOTION	F	G

F: Facts

Examining the validity of your thoughts and any underlying doubt is the most critical variable in removing doubt. The key is to learn to collect, digest, and accept the facts. Some of us can be objective about our own thoughts and are able to avoid letting our emotions color our perceptions. Others let our emotions skyrocket out of control and thus lose objectivity; those emotions interfere with our ability to think rationally, clearly, and logically. You can learn to examine the truth of your thoughts and not let your emotions bias your perspective.

It's time to look for the facts. The facts will lead you to see whether your distress is warranted or not. Unwarranted distress is always connected to erroneous perceptions driven by erroneous doubt. Your distress came from your perception of the activating event not the event itself. Your perception is what we call your *cognitions* in the Doubt Register. Now it is time to examine the truth of your perceptions.

To examine the facts, you need to follow these steps:

1. See if the facts support or disconfirm your perceptions.

2. Regardless of whether your perceptions are true or not, see if the facts directly support your doubt label.

Here is a pool of potential questions available to guide you to the facts. You might find one question is enough, or might need two or the whole list. There is no special order you need to follow; the key is to keep asking questions until all the facts are uncovered.

- What is the actual danger? Am I exaggerating the threat or its effect on me? Am I overestimating the likelihood of the danger occurring or overestimating the damage?

- What is the worst thing that can happen?

- What is the best thing that can happen?

- What is the most likely to happen?

- Can I handle the problem? What are all the assets I'm equipped with?

Hint: *Think about all the assets within you: knowledge, experience, humor, personality, intellect, savvy, problem-solving skills, and confidence. Then think of all the assets outside of you: friends, significant others, family, colleagues, neighbors, coaches, teachers, and clergy.*

- What is the proof for and against my thought?

- Are my thoughts completely true, partly true, or do they possess a grain of truth?

- What are some other possibilities that explain the situation?

- What would a friend tell me?

- What would I tell a friend?

Remember, it is your interpretation of an event that affects you and not the event itself. Sam and Jill applied facts to their thoughts and entered them into their Doubt Registers.

Can You Relate to Sam?

Looking for the facts, Sam sees situations through an objective lens. Thinking about an upcoming business event, he realizes how much he knows based on his expertise. When a friend gives him unsolicited advice, instead of automatically concluding his competence is being questioned, he sees the facts. His facts are listed on the Doubt Registers on pages 75 and 76 .

ACTIVATING SITUATION (SAM)	BODY RESPONSE	COGNITIONS	DOUBT LABEL	EMOTION	FACTS	G
Thinking about an upcoming meeting.	Aroused, heart rate escalated.	Someone is going to ask me a question to trip me up.	I'm incompetent.	Anger, hurt, fear.	Most people are half-asleep and not knowledgeable enough to even ask me a question. How can anyone trip me up when I know more details, more facts, and more technical data than anyone else in the room? There are no facts here to support the idea that I'm incompetent.	

ACTIVATING SITUATION (SAM)	BODY RESPONSE	COGNITIONS	DOUBT LABEL	EMOTION	FACTS	G
A friend gives him unsolicited advice (while playing cards or golf, for example).	Aroused, blood boiling, face flushed, muscles tensed, pulse throbbing.	Who are you to give me advice? You should not be giving me advice. You're questioning my competency.	I'm incompetent.	Rage.	I have been playing golf and cards with these guys for years. They know how good I am, so it is possible they are not insulting me. Maybe they genuinely think they are helping or being a good friend. I would rather they didn't give me advice, but they can't stop themselves. There are no facts here that say I am incompetent.	

Can You Relate to Jill?

Blind to the facts, Jill thought her date would find her unattractive and unappealing. Looking through the lens of objectivity, the truth is in the facts. The data shows that people find her attractive and appealing, and they tell her so. When a man calls her two hours later than he said he would, she automatically thinks she is unattractive and he is no longer interested. The facts clearly demonstrate that there is no evidence for her doubt. The facts are recorded on Jill's Doubt Registers on pages 78 and 79.

Your Turn

In Sam's and Jill's Doubt Registers, you can see how the facts contradicted the validity of the upsetting thoughts. Once the thoughts were found to be untrue, the falseness of the doubts was apparent. Now it's your turn. Use the questions listed earlier to find the facts and uncover the truth regarding your thoughts and your doubt. Write your facts in your Doubt Register.

ACTIVATING SITUATION (JILL)	BODY RESPONSE	COGNITIONS	DOUBT LABEL	EMOTION	FACTS	G
Getting ready for her blind date.	Tired, nausea.	He will find me unattractive. He will think I am unappealing.	I'm unlovable.	Sad, hopeless.	He already finds me amusing at some level because we have had so many funny conversations. Although I don't see it, my friends, my colleagues, and my aunts tell me I am attractive. Even if he doesn't find me attractive, so what? He is single and looking, so who is he to judge. Lots of men have found me appealing, and it is possible he will, too. Maybe we will like each other, or maybe I won't like him. Either way, it is just a night out. What do I have to lose? There is no support for my being unlovable.	

ACTIVATING SITUATION (JILL)	BODY RESPONSE	COGNITIONS	DOUBT LABEL	EMOTION	FACTS	G
A man calls two hours later than he said he would.	Fatigue, agitated, nervous.	He thinks I am unattractive. He's not interested. I am undesirable.	I'm not good enough to be loved. I'm unlovable.	Sad, anxious.	He already told me he is looking forward to our next date, and we are scheduled to see each other Friday. He told me I am beautiful, and the last time we were together he kept staring at me all night. He does have a long commute, and maybe he isn't home yet. It's possible he had something to do and will call later. Even if he does not call tonight, it does not mean he is not interested, it may just mean he was unavailable to make the call. Either way, there are no real facts that say I am not good enough for him to love.	

ACTIVATING SITUATION (YOU)	BODY RESPONSE	COGNITIONS	DOUBT LABEL	EMOTION	FACTS	G

G: Go Time

Go time is the opportunity to put it all together. First, look at all of the facts, summarize them, and *rethink* the conclusion. Knowing doubt was unfounded means you recognize you are equipped to handle whatever concern you are facing. You have concluded you can count on yourself and if you need help, it is out there. Armed with this confidence you can now *relax*. Your distress is shrinking, and that means you will have energy to *respond* in the most productive way possible. Without doubt, your actions will be more effective. By using the *go time* skill, you will now face such situations fortified with confidence.

Ask yourself:

- Am I equipped to handle it?

- What assets do I bring to the situation?

Can You Relate to Sam?
After Sam reviewed the facts, the meeting he dreaded no longer seemed a threat. The unsolicited advice seemed trivial, and he saw that his upset was disproportionate to the problem. His Doubt Registers on pages 83 and 84 show his conclusions.

Can You Relate to Jill?
After reviewing the facts, Jill concluded her fears that her blind date would find her unattractive and undesirable and that a late phone call was a sign of rejection were unfounded. She recorded conclusions in her Doubt Registers on pages 85 and 86.

Your Turn

Now it is your turn. Finish your Doubt Register by writing in your conclusions. Make sure to talk back to your doubt and let the facts rule.

ACTIVATING SITUATION (SAM)	BODY RESPONSE	COGNITIONS	DOUBT LABEL	EMOTION	FACTS	GO TIME: RETHINK, RELAX, RESPOND
Thinking about an upcoming meeting.	Aroused, heart rate escalated.	Someone is going to ask me a question to trip me up.	I'm incompetent.	Anger, hurt, fear.	Most people are half-asleep and not knowledgeable enough to even ask me a question. How can anyone trip me up when I know more details, more facts, and more technical data than anyone else in the room? There are no facts here to support the idea that I'm incompetent.	*Rethink:* My concerns that people are going to trip me up are (1) so unlikely to occur and (2) so unlikely to be a problem that there is no reason for alarm. I am competent. It was my doubt getting in the way. *Relax:* I notice I am calmer and a lot less angry, hurt, and fearful. *Respond:* Enter the meeting feeling confident and with vigor in my walk.

ACTIVATING SITUATION (SAM)	BODY RESPONSE	COGNITIONS	DOUBT LABEL	EMOTION	FACTS	GO TIME: RETHINK, RELAX, RESPOND
A friend gives him unsolicited advice (while playing cards or golf, for example).	Aroused, blood boiling, face flushed, muscles tensed, pulse throbbing.	Who are you to give me advice? You should not be giving me advice. You're questioning my competency.	I'm incompetent.	Rage.	I have been playing golf and cards with these guys for years. They know how good I am, so it is possible they are not insulting me. Maybe they genuinely think they are helping or being a good friend. I would rather they didn't give me advice but they can't stop themselves. There are no facts here that say I am incompetent.	*Rethink:* My friends are exactly that, my friends. They are not out to get me. I am super-competent in these things, and my concern is that they were insulting my skill was unfounded. Doubt was getting in the way of recognizing not only that I am competent but that others see me this way, too. *Relax:* The muscle tension is less, and my anger is subsiding. *Respond:* Smile and ignore the advice. Next time I am not going to let it get to me.

ACTIVATING SITUATION (JILL)	BODY RESPONSE	COGNITIONS	DOUBT LABEL	EMOTION	FACTS	GO TIME: RETHINK, RELAX, RESPOND
Getting ready for her blind date.	Tired, nausea.	He will find me unattractive. He will think I am unappealing.	I'm unlovable.	Sad, hopeless.	He already finds me amusing at some level because we have had so many funny conversations. Although I don't see it, my friends, my colleagues, and my aunts tell me I am attractive. Even if he doesn't find me attractive, so what? He is single and looking, so who is he to judge. Lots of men have found me appealing, and it is possible he will too. Maybe we will like each other, or maybe I won't like him. Either way it is just a night out. What do I have to lose. There is no support for my being unlovable.	*Rethink:* The facts support that I am an attractive person. It is my unreasonable unlovability doubt that tells me I won't be good enough. I am lovable, and I have plenty of people in my life who care about me to prove it. *Relax:* I feel encouraged and notice maybe I am not that tired. *Respond:* Go on the date without being preoccupied with interfering doubt.

ACTIVATING SITUATION (JILL)	BODY RESPONSE	COGNITIONS	DOUBT LABEL	EMOTION	FACTS	GO TIME: RETHINK, RELAX, RESPOND
A man calls her two hours later than he said he would.	Fatigue, agitated, nervous.	He thinks I am unattractive. He's not interested. I am undesirable.	I'm not good enough to be loved. I'm unlovable.	Sad, anxious.	He has already told me he is looking forward to our next date, and we are scheduled to see each other Friday. He told me I am beautiful, and the last time we were together he kept starring at me all night. He does have a long commute, and maybe he isn't home yet. It's possible he had something to do and will call later. Even if he does not call tonight, it does not mean he is not interested, it may just mean he was unavailable to make the call. Either way, there are no real facts that I am not good enough for him to love.	*Rethink:* This guy is clearly interested. It is my irrational unlovability doubt that sees rejection. I am good enough and lovable, even if this guy does not wind up loving me. *Relax:* I notice I feel calmer. *Respond:* Go take a bath and start a new book.

ACTIVATING SITUATION (YOU)	BODY RESPONSE	COGNITIONS	DOUBT LABEL	EMOTION	FACTS	GO TIME: RETHINK, RELAX, RESPOND

The Bottom Line

In this chapter, you learned how to deconstruct doubt. We worked on building your examination skills. First, you learned how to pay attention and record body responses, cognitions, doubt, and emotions in response to your activating situations. Next, you learned to distinguish between realistic concern and doubt. You also learned that if your emotions were too intense, timed time-outs help you move away from emotional thinking to logical thinking. Then, you learned how to systematically examine the facts by using specific questions to differentiate between faulty interpretations that cement doubt and facts that show you the truth. You then were able to realistically understand your vulnerability in comparison to your internal and external assets. By learning the ABCs of doubt, you learned to take the power away from doubt and to rethink, relax, and then respond effectively.

Chapter Four

Recognize Doubt Distortions and Throw Them Out

Doubt starts as a tiny seed that steadily and slowly, under the right conditions, grows inside of you. It transforms and shapes the way you view yourself, until one day you look in the mirror and no longer recognize who you thought you could become. Doubt can transform your internal appearance from the once-confident individual to one who is often consumed with hesitation, self-criticism, and second-guessing. The fertilizer for doubt is your perception.

Perception is the way we make sense of ourselves, our relationships, and the world. Because it is impossible for any of us to pay attention to everything going on around us, we develop a filtering system as a way of interpreting information. As is the problem with any type of filter, our system allows only certain information to pass through. Over time, the filter becomes more restrictive, distorting our perception in consistent ways. Eventually, we fail to see the big picture because we no longer receive alternative information. We may be missing real or positive information from the actual event, feedback from others, or even our own internal opinions.

So what exactly is a *doubt distortion*? A doubt distortion is a thinking mistake. It is your personal thinking style, which filters how you interpret everything going on around and inside you in the same way repeatedly. This leads you to see the world and yourself inaccurately. Over time, you tend to unknowingly view the world and yourself from this consistently rigid, inaccurate perspective. This biased way of seeing the world and yourself becomes a bad habit in that you automatically process information based on the main doubt distortions you use. As a result, you stop allowing yourself to see things in an objective, realistic way. Doubt activation and stress tend to exacerbate our bad habits, including our distorted filtering systems. Distortions can bias the way we remember the past, interpret the present, and predict the future.

We all make doubt distortions at times, but some of us fall into the habit of using them more often than not. Seeing the world through the doubt-distorted lens leads us to process information incorrectly. Instead of seeing the truth, we draw inaccurate conclusions of what is going on around us and inside of us. Typical doubt distortions are dichotomizing, emotional relying, nasty name calling, snowballing, crystal balling, demanding, and pause button pressing. Each of us uses some of these distortions more than others. Which one or ones are you in the habit of making? The following discussion will help you decide.

Dichotomizing

Imagine you take someone out for a business lunch. You arrive several minutes late and find that the person you are meeting is already waiting for you at the table. As you approach, you are mentally checking the failure boxes next to being on time and making a good first impression. You are trying to make your sales quota for the month. You can feel your mood and conversation style are affected by the nagging thought that you already blew the sale. Despite your concerns, the meeting lasts longer than you expected, and your customer asks lots of questions. At the end of lunch, he thanks you for setting up the meeting and exits the restaurant without committing to the sale. *Did you really completely blow it by arriving late?*

Disadvantages of Dichotomizing

The difficulty with dichotomizing is you see things as being only one way or the other rather than in shades of gray or on a continuum. You see yourself as either a success or a failure, smart or stupid, winner or loser, good or bad.

What are the negatives to having the dichotomizing habit? If you think about it, your world becomes very small when you lump everything you say, do, try, think, or accomplish into one of only two boxes, the good box or the bad box. To do this, you also need to develop and apply rigid standards because there is no continuum. There is no room for improvement or a pat on the back as you get closer to your goal. There are only the end points.

It is okay to want to be your best. You just need to see that to get there requires hard work as you slowly move your way up the continuum. Imagine trying to lose weight or beginning an exercise regimen and never giving yourself any credit for progress. Develop a new habit of seeing what you think, feel, and as being somewhere on a continuum. Sue is a single female in her thirties who has struggled with slow weight gain for the last fifteen years. She would never be able to make healthy changes in her diet or begin to exercise if she saw only the finish line. When she first started using the elliptical machine, it was for five minutes each time, but a year later she can stay on it for forty-five minutes. Confidence comes from finding meaning in the gray area.

Can You Relate to Dale?

One of Dale's favorite doubt distortions is dichotomizing. He wakes up in the morning, and if something goes wrong, he is in for a bad day. A bad start to the day colors how he interacts with his family, his ride to work, and his workday. Before he knows it, the whole day is bad. The dichotomizing doubt distortion is at the root because it has filtered out all the positive information. Unknowingly, Dale is less effective at work, more short-tempered with those around him, and definitely not on his game. The facts are that there are upsets in our day, things that don't go quite the way we plan, problems, and stressors, *but* that does not mean that everything else must be lumped into the bad category as well. The key is to place each area of life on its own continuum and to treat them all separately.

BE A DOUBT DETECTIVE: DO YOU USE TOO MUCH DICHOTOMIZING?

Do you tend to agree with the following statements?

- There are only two categories: good and bad.

- There is no gray area.

- If you don't reach a specific standard of success, then you fail.

- If one thing goes wrong, then it is all wrong.

- I can only succeed or fail.

Or do you tend to agree with these statements?

- Categories are merely points on a continuum.

- I give myself credit for each step toward my overall goal.

- Every point on the continuum provides rich information from which to learn and build.

- There is no such thing as all wrong or all right, complete failure or complete success, or totally bad or totally good.

- I give myself a pat on the back for effort and any small gain.

SELF-ANALYSIS
If you tend to agree with the first set of statements, you depend too much on dichotomizing.

If you do not use dichotomizing all the time, then you tend to agree more with the second set of statements, which are alternative, nondistorted ways of looking at your world. Living without doubt necessitates striving to see the world on a continuum and not as a category.

If you find yourself dichotomizing, remember to live life on a continuum and find meaning from wherever you land. Get rid of the good box and the bad box.

Emotional Relying

Picture yourself relaxing on the back of a friend's boat. Another boat has tied up to yours and everyone is having lunch together. You get the impression that the couple from the other boat does not like you. You may feel diminished or dismissed or just have a negative vibe. *Is that feeling an accurate reflection of what the others truly think?*

Disadvantages of Emotional Relying

When we make conclusions based on feelings alone, we are participating in emotional relying. What are some of the disadvantages to emotional relying? Feelings supply important pieces of information and should not be ignored. However, feelings are unreliable data sources because of their subjectivity and ability to be influenced by multitudes of variables outside of our control. When we say that feelings are subjective, we mean they are not fact driven. With emotional relying, we let our feelings guide us, regardless of the facts of the given situation. Often the facts contradict our feelings, and yet we still let our emotions win.

Feelings are quite susceptible to manipulation by outside factors. How we feel can change in a moment. You walk outside, and the weather is perfect, the sun is shining, a warm breeze is blowing, and you notice a lift in your mood and in your step. Now consider that you walk outside and the rain is pelting you in the face, the wind is whipping you, and the air is cold. Your mood sinks, and your energy disappears. How about when someone tells you, "You look terrific today" or "Your paper was brilliant" or "You look tired"; do you notice that your mood rises or sinks accordingly? Feelings are just that, feelings. Basing our judgment solely on them allows us to draw faulty conclusions that encourage doubt.

Do you believe in intuition? Sure intuition can be a guide, just like feelings, but let your emotions be only one source of information. Instead fortify the validity of your feelings with facts. Facts are reliable and valid information that cannot be denied. Develop the new habit of being fact driven instead of feeling driven, and be free of the destructive damage of emotional relying.

Can You Relate to Erin?

Consider Erin who depends too much on emotional relying. She feels fat, ugly, and unwanted. She takes these thoughts at face value, allowing them to sink her mood and guide her choices of action. Feeling fat and ugly, her mood sinks, and she elects not to join her friends at the dance club. Sitting home alone, Erin now feels that she is unwanted and allows that feeling to ruin her night and lead her to the wrong conclusions. Had Erin looked at the facts, her mood and her behavior would have been different. The reality is that she is an attractive woman whose friends want her to join them. The facts are she is a size eight, considered a small size on anyone's measure and as far from fat as possible. Her beauty and long silky luxuriant hair, smooth tan complexion, large dark eyes, radiant smile, and tone figure are regarded by our society as assets. The facts are her friends begged her to join them and are always asking her to participate in their fun. Had Erin reminded herself of the facts, her mood would not have sunk, and she would have chosen a night of dancing instead of a night of feeling unwanted at home.

BE A DOUBT DETECTIVE: DO YOU USE TOO MUCH EMOTIONAL RELYING?

Do you tend to agree with the following statements?

- I focus on my feelings.

- If it feels true, it must be true.

- One can count on one's intuition.

- Feelings are what are most important.

- Feelings guide my decisions.

Or do you tend to agree with these statements?

- I look for the facts.

- What matters are the facts.

- Feelings are important but are only one source of information.

- Facts are indisputable and reliable.

- Facts are the best source of information in making decisions.

SELF-ANALYSIS

If you tend to agree with the first set of statements, you depend too much on emotional relying.

If you do not use emotional relying all the time, then you tend to agree more with the second set of statements, which offer alternative, nondistorted ways of looking at your world. Living without doubt means striving to see the world through a fact-based lens.

To avoid emotional relying, focus on the facts of the situation and not your feelings. Be fact driven and not feeling driven.

Nasty Name Calling

Imagine you walk up in front of a large group of people to begin your presentation. Everyone is seated, and you begin. After about ten minutes into the presentation, you begin to scan the room. You notice that some people are paying attention, whereas others seem to be doodling or checking their PDAs. The worst offenders in your eyes are the ones that quietly whisper to each other. Your interpretation is that you have been branded by them as "boring," "not engaging," or "not good enough." You label the crowd as "rude" and "disinterested." You feel irritated, frustrated, and anxious. *Are these labels for yourself and the audience accurate?*

Disadvantages of Nasty Name Calling
Nasty name calling is a global negative judgment you make about yourself. What are some of the many disadvantages associated with nasty name calling? When you call yourself names, you let doubt take over and shape the way you view yourself. The label you have for yourself and others tends to be negative. Rather than being able to refer to a specific action or behavior that you would like to try to improve or learn from, you tend to brand yourself in a negative way and give up. The nasty name calling may shape how you view yourself, and you may generalize it across the board to new situations. You may also call others names and never give them a chance to be part of your life. Using nasty name calling on yourself and others creates a negative environment, which further cements doubt and squashes confidence.

Take the situation in which Joe tries to recork a bottle of red wine but accidentally spills half the bottle on his friend's beige sport jacket. He thinks, "Idiot." We can learn from the name calling by dissecting it and recognizing that the mess up was a simple mistake that did not warrant the label Joe gave it. Instead of focusing on the accident, Joe can remember the great time they had at dinner and how his friend made light of the stain on his jacket. Then, we also can give ourselves credit for the positive aspects.

Can You Relate to John?

John is meeting his friend for coffee and is at the counter ordering. He tells the woman he'd like regular coffee. She then asks him what flavor and what size he wants. He filters the situation to mean, "I'm stupid." As he takes his coffee to the fixing bar, he places it down a little too hard and it spills. He interprets this as another piece of information that he is stupid. This serves to further cement the doubt label of not measuring up. As his friend approaches, he says, "I'm usually the one wearing stains on my shirt." The fact is that everyone spills at some point, and it is no big deal. Some of us are just able to laugh it off and dismiss any negative thoughts about it immediately.

BE A DOUBT DETECTIVE: DO YOU USE TOO MUCH NASTY NAME CALLING?

Do you tend to agree with the following statements?

- I label my actions with name calling.

- If I call myself a nasty name that label must be true.

- If I call someone else a nasty name that label must be true.

- In all situations, my nasty name gets triggered.

- The nasty name is my identity.

Or do you tend to agree with these statements?

- I examine and review my actions without sticking a nasty name on them.

- Calling myself nasty names is likely to lead me to believe the validity of those names.

- It is more accurate to describe someone else's upsetting behavior than it is to call him or her a nasty name.

- Regardless of my mistakes, I refrain from calling myself nasty names.

- Lots of characteristics make up how I define myself.

SELF-ANALYSIS

If you tend to agree with the first set of statements, you depend too much on nasty name calling.

If you do not use nasty name calling all the time, then you tend to agree more with the second set of statements, which offer alternative nondistorted ways of looking at your world. Living without doubt means moving away from using nasty name calling on ourselves and others.

To avoid being a nasty name caller, describe the specific situation without placing a label on it.

Snowballing

Imagine your fiancé asks you to marry him six weeks before you are scheduled to take an important certifying exam. He wants to get married as soon as possible, and you are thrilled. However, the excitement is overshadowed by your prediction that you will fail the certifying exam and will have to take it again four months later. You call your friends and parents and tell them very clearly that no marriage plans can be made for six months. You take the exam and start your new job the next day, convinced you failed. You imagine having to tell your boss that you failed and worry that you will get fired. Everyone at your wedding will know you failed your exam and are now unemployed. *Do you have any evidence that you will actually fail and that your entire house of cards will cave in?*

Disadvantages of Snowballing

What are some of the negatives to snowballing? You predict the outcome of each situation in the most negative way. You begin to view each situation as having a domino effect, a failure in one area will have far-reaching consequences or will affect lots of different areas of your life. You also see yourself as being extremely vulnerable and at risk for negative outcomes. You forget about the assets you bring to the equation. Snowballing leads you to believe you are in more trouble than is realistic. Perceiving danger leads you to experience anxiety or even panic and suffer needlessly. In addition, life feels as if it were a house of cards; one wrong move, and your life will completely crumble, leading to terror and despair. We refer to this bad habit as snowballing because this doubt distortion is like a snowball at the top of the mountain that gathers strength, speed, and size as it rolls down this hill and causes quite a bit of destruction to anything in its path.

Do you believe in examining as many reasonable outcomes as possible? Doing so makes sense and will make you a better problem solver. However, it is important not to get stuck on the most negative possible outcome, which is usually more catastrophic than is realistic. Instead, use the facts to shore up the assets you bring to the situation. Develop the new habit of examining the full range of potential outcomes rather concentrating on the excessive and most negative outcome.

Can You Relate to Mary?

Mary is leaving to go on a cruise with her friend. As she and her friend are boarding the boat, a man says to her friend, "I hope to see you a lot over the next week." Suddenly, Mary notices that her mood begins to sour, and she starts to envision herself going to activities alone and being thankful that room service is free. She imagines her friend will leave her after she meets up with this guy, and she will have the absolute worst time on the cruise because she will be alone for meals, activities, and excursions. The facts are that her long-time friend has never chosen a man over her, and the guy did not even ask that they meet. He may also be with a friend, so the four of them could all have a good time together. Or maybe he was just making small talk.

BE A DOUBT DETECTIVE: DO YOU USE TOO MUCH SNOWBALLING?

Do you tend to agree with the following statements?

- I focus on the most negative possible outcome.

- There is no best-case scenario or realistic outcome.

- If something goes wrong, it will have disastrous consequences.

- Difficulties snowball out of control.

- My risks far outweigh my assets.

Or do you tend to agree with these statements?

- I try to examine the worst, best, and most realistic possible outcomes.

- Usually, the most realistic outcome or some derivation of that occurs.

- Difficulties are just that, difficulties.

- After the situation is assessed, I can figure out which assets to use.

- The facts are that my assets usually far outweigh my risks.

SELF-ANALYSIS

If you tend to agree with the first set of statements, you depend too much on snowballing.

If you do not use snowballing all the time, then you tend to agree with the second set of statements, which offer alternative, nondistorted ways of looking at your world. Living without doubt means striving to see the world through this realistic risk and asset lens.

To avoid snowballing, focus on the specific facts of the situations and not the worst possible outcome. Consider the most likely outcome.

Crystal Balling

Imagine you are sitting at the airport waiting at the gate to take an early morning flight for a business meeting. The airline representative announces that there are storms in the area where you are headed, and you will be delayed at least an hour. It is too early to call your client, and you predict it will mess up his whole day. You begin to imagine that this will put him in a terrible mood and negatively affect your meeting. You then use crystal balling to predict that you will not be able to close the deal. *Do you have any evidence that your client will not understand that your tardiness was due to factors outside your control?*

Disadvantages of Crystal Balling

The difficulty with crystal balling is that you think you can predict the outcome of your actions or events, and the bias is typically in the negative direction. What are some of the many disadvantages to crystal balling? The truth is that no one owns a crystal ball. It is important to accept that it is not possible to predict the future, and in trying to do so you are causing yourself needless distress. Think about all the possible outcomes of any given situation. Can you guarantee which outcome will result? Typically not, as there are always variables out of your control that will play a role in what happens. The problem is not only that you operate as if you could predict the future but that you make your prediction in only the negative direction. Instead of imagining the best or most likely outcome, you assume that a negative outcome is most typical. Instead of thinking you could have a good time at a party, you assume you won't. Instead of thinking your presentation will be well received, you assume it will be awful.

Breaking the habit of crystal balling simply means forcing yourself to consider all outcomes, and not just the negative possibility. It means accepting that the future holds no guarantee. However, there are two important points to remember. One, it is likely to be not as bad as you are predicting and two, whatever it brings you have the skills to problem solve and face the challenge. Develop the new habit of staying in the present and not falsely predicting the future.

Can You Relate to Brett?

Brett has been invited to a company golf outing to play on his boss's foursome. His boss is counting on him to help the team take the prize. He sets up on the first tee and swings; his drive fades left, landing him in a deep sand trap. Brett thinks, "This is going to be a terrible round, they are counting on me, and I am going to let everyone down." His mood sinks, and he gets himself into a bad mood as he walks to his next shot. Crystal balling has the potential of ruining his entire round and maximizing the chance that his negative prediction will actually come true. Instead, Brett can teach himself to recognize that this is only one shot out of ninety. He can remind himself that anything can happen in a golf game, but the bottom line is that he is a good golfer and he has lots of time to be the asset to his team he most likely will be.

BE A DOUBT DETECTIVE: DO YOU USE TOO MUCH CRYSTAL BALLING?

Do you tend to agree with the following statements?

- I just know the future will be bad.

- I never consider the best outcome.

- I can predict the future based on the vibe I get from the situation.

- I just know how things will turn out.

- I rarely think about what is most likely to happen.

Or do you tend to agree with these statements?

- I know there is always the possibility that the future will be good.

- I let myself consider the best outcome.

- I wait for the outcome rather than predict it.

- I know that I cannot predict the future.

- I remind myself of what is most likely to happen.

SELF-ANALYSIS

If you tend to agree with the first set of statements, you depend too much on crystal balling.

If you do not use crystal balling all the time, then you tend to agree with the second set of statements, which offer alternative, nondistorted ways of looking at your world. Living without doubt means not using a crystal ball.

To avoid crystal balling, don't try to forecast the future. Instead, consider the best and most likely outcomes.

The Demandings

Imagine you arrive home from work later than you expected. You had planned to make an elaborate dinner for you and your boyfriend. Although it will take you a long time and much effort, you decide to proceed with your plan. Wilting from exhaustion, you tell yourself you have to do this or your evening will be compromised. As you painstakingly prepare the food, you feel frustrated and angry that your boyfriend has not volunteered to help. Instead of asking him to help or considering reasonable explanations for why he is unavailable (such as collecting wood for a nice fire or finishing up his work so that he has the rest of the evening free), you think he should be helping. The questions are: Is it absolutely necessary that you make the elaborate dinner? Is it reasonable to demand that your boyfriend help without your asking him to?

Think about when you first wake up in the morning. Do you say, "This is the beginning of another day and start fresh!" or does your brain suddenly jump into action with all the shoulds, have-tos, and need-tos for the day? Demanding yourself or others into action leads only to frustration and being overwhelmed before you even begin. The demandings place an unrealistic amount of pressure on you and trigger doubt. Confidence is squelched under the strain of your expectations. Anger and upset toward others can increase when they do not live up to your demandings of them. The demandings put constant pressure on yourself and others to perform according to rigid imperatives. *Does everything absolutely have to get done in the rigidly unrealistic time frame you have set for yourself?*

Disadvantages of the Demandings

The disadvantage of the demandings is that you put constant pressure on yourself and others to be better or to achieve. The rub is that not only do you stress yourself with unrealistic and constant demands but that you tend to have the same standards for others. This tends to put a strain on your relationships and increases your anxiety, panic, and frustration. As mentioned earlier, the demandings are usually in the form of musts, have-tos, need-tos, ought-tos, and shoulds. Through the demandings, life is a constant drain because there is the constant weight of what has yet to be accomplished.

The demandings we place on others are often unfulfilled, resulting in disappointment, frustration, and irritation. Thinking they should, could, ought, must, and need assumes we have control of the world around us. Accepting you have zero control over others is necessary to stop the demandings. Although you can prefer, wish, or desire them to do or not do certain things, you cannot demand it of them. Life can be more fully enjoyed when you let go of the demandings. You can live life frustration free.

Amy thinks after years of telling her kids to do their chores and their homework, they should take the initiative and do it without having to be told. Simply demanding it of them, however, does not increase the likelihood of it actually happening. Telling herself that she wishes her kids would be more responsible and compliant makes it easier for her to problem solve how to maximize making that happen. Develop the new habit of putting the demandings into a realistic perspective and change the demandings into wishes or desires. In terms of others, try to be realistic about what they are able to accomplish and recognize demanding that it happen does not make it any more likely to happen.

Can You Relate to Lisa?

Lisa is out to dinner with a group of other women. Everyone has just ordered dessert, and Lisa thinks, "I should not have dessert," but orders it anyway. She then feels angry at herself for not having more discipline. Later that night, Lisa feels insulted by her sister who has told her she does not have as much to do as she does, and so Lisa should be the one to take their mother to the doctor. Lisa feels hurt and thinks, "I shouldn't be so sensitive, I shouldn't let her get to me, I should have been more assertive and said I have plenty to do, I can't do it." Lisa constantly places demands on herself, which means she always feels disappointed in herself, which in turn reinforces her doubt that she is not good enough.

BE A DOUBT DETECTIVE: DO YOU USE TOO MUCH DEMANDING?

Do you tend to agree with the following statements?

- Others should do what I expect.

- It is reasonable for me to place demands on myself.

- It is reasonable for me to place demands on others.

- Others should just know what needs to be done.

- I should be able to adhere to my demands.

Or do you tend to agree with these statements?

- It would be nice if others did what I expect, but I can't demand it.

- I can't make demands of myself, I can only try my best.

- I can't make demands of others, I can only ask for what I want.

- I can't expect others to know what I wish without communicating it clearly to them.

- It would be nice if I adhered to my demands but I can only try.

SELF-ANALYSIS

If you tend to agree with the first set of statements, you depend too much on the demandings.

If you do not use the demandings all the time, then you tend to agree with the second set of statements, which offer alternative, nondistorted ways of looking at your world. Living without doubt means wishing, preferring, or communicating rather than using the demandings.

To avoid demandings, prefer, plan, or communicate instead.

Pause Button Pressing

Imagine you are a character in your own movie and during your dinner party you press the pause button. The still image is on the screen. What do you see? Do you look around you and see the food left on everyone's plates and the vegetable soufflé you spent hours making left untouched? Do you see the red wine stains on your tablecloth and the crooked picture on the wall? Do you perceive boredom in the person sitting across from you? Or do you see the whole picture, including the chicken and salad that have been devoured, the happy grins on the faces of several guests, the beautiful flower arrangement at the center of the table, and everyone eying the seven-layer chocolate cake that is waiting to be served? Pause button pressing happens when the person who stops the film ignores the neutral and positive information and focuses exclusively on the negatives. The person who uses pause button pressing minimizes the positives and magnifies the negatives. *Can you see anything positive in the still picture on your screen?*

Disadvantages of Pause Button Pressing
When negative images are magnified, you form exaggerated, non-constructive conclusions. Ignoring, minimizing, and discounting positive information across situations creates a biased filter that leads one to draw faulty conclusions. These faulty conclusions provide ammunition for doubt.

Tom is the proprietor of a large medical practice and usually arrives at the office a half hour after his office staff. Upon arriving, he notices piles of unfiled charts, magazines in disarray around the waiting room, the phones set to the answering service, and his staff away from the front desk huddled in the back of the office. He thinks to himself that he is not paying them to goof off and that the office is doomed to be unprofitable. What he fails to notice is the three patients already waiting in exam rooms, the thirty charts already filed, and one calamity avoided. Pause button pressing is the distorted view. By using it, Tom focuses on the negatives and ignores the positives.

Pause button pressing encourages doubt by magnifying the negatives and minimizing the positives, ending in faulty, pessimistic conclusions. This biased perspective influences your actions, often leading you to harmful or unhelpful behavior. Seeing the accurate whole picture is necessary if you are to avoid inaccurate assumptions and destructive behaviors.

Focusing on and exaggerating the negatives also results in unnecessary emotional pain. Not only can it sink your mood but it can cause you troublesome anxiety when you think of the imaginary danger that does not exist. The extreme negative perspective may also lead you to draw faulty conclusions about yourself, which often confirm your doubt label.

Ignoring and making light of the positives can also confirm doubt. Failing to see the positives interferes with opportunities to give yourself credit. When you don't recognize your accomplishments, you allow your negative self-image to grow because you don't acknowledge the positive evidence. Forcing yourself to look at the whole picture, both the positives and the negatives, will lead to more accurate conclusions, less toxic behaviors, and the opportunity for self-esteem to grow.

Can You Relate to Mark?

Mark's inner voice constantly reminds him that he is inadequate. As a result, he regularly perceives criticism and insult that does not exist. His day is riddled with pause button pressing. Walking onto the tennis court with his wife and son, he assumes the two of them would rather play without him. On the contrary, his family wants his strong and powerful shot in the game. He overhears his wife asking his son whether he prefers to be the singles player. Mark assumes his son, who says he wants singles, wants to play alone with his mother. In truth, they were talking about Canadian doubles, in which one person must be designated as the singles player against the other two on the court. Maximizing the negative can lead us to hear and see information in distorted ways.

Later that day, Mark feels discounted when a comment he made was disregarded, when his son told him his shirt was too tight, and when his office manager reprimanded him for his hard-line way of handling an employee problem. Mark focused on all the insignificant minuses, failing to see the larger collection of pluses. He overlooked the adoration his son and his office manger have for his success and paid no attention to compliments, to the times when his advice was solicited, and when his preferences were made the priority. Because he focuses on the negatives, Mark's doubt has grown and he now tends to ignore the positives.

BE A DOUBT DETECTIVE: DO YOU USE TOO MUCH PAUSE BUTTON PRESSING?

Do you tend to agree with the following statements?

- I always focus on the negatives.

- I tend to ignore the positive information when faced with both negative and positive information.

- I tend to exaggerate negative information.

- I don't look at the whole picture.

- I downplay the positive information especially as it relates to myself.

Or do you tend to agree with these statements?

- I don't always focus on the negatives.

- I pay attention to positive information.

- I see negative information without exaggerating it.

- I look at the whole picture.

- I recognize and acknowledge positive information even if it relates to me.

SELF-ANALYSIS

If you tend to agree with the first set of statements, you depend too much on pause button pressing.

If you do not use pause button pressing all the time, then you tend to agree with the second set of statements, which offer alternative, nondistorted ways of looking at your world. Living without doubt means focusing on the big picture and seeing both the positives and the negatives through an unbiased lens.

To avoid pause button pressing, remember to see the whole picture. Try emphasizing the positives and playing down the negatives.

The Bottom Line

Doubt distortions serve to filter the information we process. These thinking mistakes lead us to draw faulty conclusions that serve to cultivate doubt. Although all of us see the world through these erroneous lenses at least once in a while, some of us tend to use these lenses more often than not. We may use one lens predominately, such as dichotomizing, or we may use a number of biased lenses all the time, such as dichotomizing, nasty name calling, and the demandings. The more we see the world through a distorted filter, the more inaccurate our perspective becomes. Such a biased and inaccurate view is a culprit in the emergence and perpetuation of doubt.

Step 3
Rethink It

Chapter Five

Rewrite Your Rules

Do you sit on the sidelines while others get in the game? Do you avoid confrontation at all costs?

Do you quit before you try? Do you give up at the first sign of stress or complication?

Do you feel the need to take control of every situation? Do you have trouble delegating?

Do you please others at a cost to yourself? Do you go overboard trying to make others happy?

Do you get easily irritated or argue with others? Do you find yourself always defending yourself?

Do you try to get others to take over or constantly seek advice or reassurance? Do you pass your responsibilities on to others?

Do you try to turn off your brain through television, music, sports, food, alcohol, or drugs instead of addressing a problem or a necessary task? Do you find things to do other than your priority?

Do you try to do everything exactly right? Do you demand perfection?

Do you dwell on all the negative possibilities? Do you imagine the worst?

If you have a strong yes reaction in response to any of these questions then it is time to rewrite your rules. To do this, you need to first pay close attention to what you typically do or how you typically respond to stressful situations. There are nine strategies that many of us typically overuse.

Let's define these strategies so we can look at what you *typically* do.

Avoid. The avoider evades, dodges, and sidesteps.

Quit. The quitter gives up, gives in, and refrains from taking action.

Control. The control freak, on the other hand, takes over and takes charge of the situation.

Please. The pleaser tries to make everyone happy by going overboard satisfying other people's needs while ignoring his or her own needs.

Defend. Defenders protect or defend themselves or attack or provoke others when they are confronted or bothered by those around them.

Delegate. The delegator passes on responsibilities or difficulties to others.

Distract. Distracters divert themselves from their priorities through television, music, sports, food, alcohol, or drugs.

Perfection. The perfectionist is meticulous, precise, demanding, and particular and is a stickler for getting things exactly right.

Worry. The worrier focuses on persistent, nagging current and potential concerns rather than on problem solving and considering other possibilities.

When you avoid falling into one of these traps, you can cope by using good problem-solving skills and following a logical plan of action. That means identifying all of the possible options and then evaluating them by looking at the advantages and disadvantages of each. You recognize that there is no one perfect choice but rather there are often multiple options that all make sense. You can then select the option that makes the most sense and implement a plan of action.

Let's try to figure out if you use one or several of these *typical* behavioral strategies.

BEHAVIORAL STRATEGIES QUIZ

Try to image each situation and then select the behavioral strategy that you would *typically* use. Circle the letter next to your choice.

1. It is a month past your due date for a review and raise. What do you do?

    A. Avoid: You won't talk to your boss and you stew every time you see him.

B. Quit: You stop putting effort into your work or you quit your job rather than having to take action.

C. Control: You take on more work responsibilities and delegate nothing.

D. Please: You work harder, going beyond reasonable limits, to please your boss.

E. Defend: You make excuses for why you do not address the issue.

F. Delegate: You ask someone you work with to let people know you are unhappy about not getting your review.

G. Distract: You focus on other things in your life and try to forget about the review.

H. Perfection: You demand more of yourself and fastidiously check your work.

I. Worry: You keep thinking, "What if I never get a raise?"

J. Problem solve and follow a plan of action: You assertively speak to the appropriate person and request a review.

2. Your friend wants you to get some friends together to celebrate her birthday. What do you do?

A. Avoid: You put off making the calls.

B. Quit: You decide it is too much for you and give up the idea.

C. Control: You take complete charge and plan every detail of the celebration, including deciding who should be invited and inviting them.

D. Please: You try to please everyone else and pick a date and a place that is not ideal for you.

E. Defend: You make excuses for why you should not be the one to handle the assignment.

F. Delegate: You call another friend and dump the task on her.

G. Distract: You put it out of your mind by getting caught up in your chores and work.

H. Perfection: You spend days deliberating on who to call and where to go.

I. Worry: You worry that no one will want to come or they will not like the arrangements you made.

J. Problem solve and follow a plan of action: You call a few of your friend's close friends and ask them to celebrate with her at her favorite restaurant.

3. You double-booked and now have two conflicting appointments. What do you do?

A. Avoid: Put off calling either appointment to correct the situation.

B. Quit: Never call either person and hope it works out.

C. Control: You take control of the situation by trying to squeeze two appointments into one slot.

D. Please: You change the time of one of the appointments but in trying to please that person you go overboard accommodating her.

E. Defend: You call one of the individuals and make lots of excuses for the double-booking.

F. Delegate: You ask your assistant to call and cancel or reschedule one of the appointments.

G. Distract: You forget about it, distracting yourself with other tasks.

H. Perfection: You beat yourself up for making the mistake.

I. Worry: You worry about the consequences of canceling or rescheduling one of the appointments and obsess over which appointment to change.

J. Problem solve and follow a plan of action: You immediately call the person whose appointment appears easiest to change and reschedule for a different time.

4. Your child has broken your house rules. What do you do?

A. Avoid: Think about the confrontation but put off addressing it.

B. Quit: Give up on your rules and let it slide.

C. Control: Type up the list of the rules and remind your child of them and/or tighten the leash and impose consequences, including less freedom.

D. Please: You try to please everyone, so you ineffectively mention the infraction but do not impose consequences.

E. Defend: You make excuses for why your child broke the rules and take no action.

F. Delegate: You tell your partner to address the issue.

G. Distract: You put off thinking about it or facing it and get involved in other things.

H. Perfection: You redefine the rules more precisely and sit down with your child, making sure he explicitly understands each rule.

I. Worry: You worry about your child's future, imagining all the horrible consequences for a kid who cannot follow the rules.

J. Problem solve and follow a plan of action: You let your child know that he has broken the rules and ask him to acknowledge what he has done wrong, apologize, and let you know how he is going to make sure it does not happen again. If the infraction, in your opinion, is significant, you impose a penalty.

5. You have taken a new job and are told that you will receive training so you can tackle more complex tasks and earn more money. Months go by, and you still have not received the training. What do you do?

   A. Avoid: You do nothing and wait for the opportunity to be presented to you.

   B. Quit: Your quit the job in frustration over not being given the opportunity.

   C. Control: You obtain a copy of the employee handbook and your contract and look for ways in which written policy can help you take control of the situation.

   D. Please: You work even harder trying to please everyone at work, hoping it will pay off.

   E. Defend: You believe they are denying you this opportunity because of your shortcomings and make excuses for any difficulties at work.

   F. Delegate: You find someone else who started around the time you did and tell her to plead both of your cases to get training.

   G. Distract: You busy yourself in your work and forget about any promises.

   H. Perfection: You work harder, checking and rechecking your work for mistakes, trying to be perfect so that you will get results.

I. Worry: You worry you will never get the training and never get the raise.

J. Problem solve and follow a plan of action: You assertively approach the appropriate person and ask when the training can be scheduled.

6. You had a confrontation with a person whom you are likely to see at another event you are planning to attend. What do you do?

   A. Avoid: You do not go to the event so that you won't have to face him.

   B. Quit: You go to the event and the minute you see him, you leave.

   C. Control: You elicit the help of others to keep you surrounded and away from this person.

   D. Please: You go out of your way to be nice to this person.

   E. Defend: You plead your case to other individuals who are going so they will take your side.

   F. Delegate: You get one of your friends to talk to this person and smooth things over.

   G. Distract: You have a drink and focus on the food and music.

   H. Perfection: You practice what you are going to say to this person over and over.

   I. Worry: You dread seeing him, fearing another confrontation.

   J. Problem solve and follow a plan of action: You decide to go to the event, say hello to this person, and walk away free to enjoy the evening.

7. A pile of necessary paperwork arrives in the mail. What do you do?

   A. Avoid: You put it in a pile on the back of the counter and walk away from it.

   B. Quit: You start to look at it and immediately put it away.

   C. Control: You sort through the paperwork and make a plan to get it done.

   D. Please: You let someone else's needs be the priority and put the paperwork off.

   E. Defend: You make excuses for why you cannot get to the paperwork.

   F. Delegate: You ask someone else to do the paperwork.

   G. Distract: You toss it aside and watch television, read a book, or find something else to occupy yourself.

   H. Perfection: You spend hours meticulously completing the paperwork and take additional time to review what you have completed.

   I. Worry: You worry you will never get to the paperwork or you won't be able to complete it.

   J. Problem solve and follow a plan of action: You schedule time to get the paperwork done and efficiently complete it.

8. You are looking forward to driving with a friend and she informs you she wants to drive separately. What do you do?

   A. Avoid: Say nothing and drive your own car.

B. Quit: You decide not to go unless someone else volunteers to drive you.

C. Control: You call other friends until you find someone else to drive with you.

D. Please: You assure your friend that it is no big deal and you understand.

E. Defend: You find reasons for why she doesn't want to drive with you.

F. Delegate: You ask another friend to persuade this friend to drive with you.

G. Distract: You try not to think about it.

H. Perfection: You drive yourself after meticulously researching a driving route and programming it into your navigation system.

I. Worry: You worry you will not find your way on your own or you worry you have done something wrong.

J. Problem solve and follow a plan of action: You acknowledge your disappointment and choose to drive alone or find another friend to drive with.

SELF-ANALYSIS

Look at the letter you circled for each example. Did you tend to circle one letter more than the others? Can you see a pattern? Are you likely to avoid, quit, be a control freak, please others, defend yourself, delegate, distract, be a perfectionist, worry, or problem solve? The behavioral strategy or strategies you engage in are linked to self-doubt. For example, the control freak demands control to reduce discomfort. Not having control activates a sense of powerlessness. This is especially true in situations in which the person feels victimized or taken advantage of. Feeling powerless activates doubt about being capable. The label of this doubt might be "I'm powerless," "I'm helpless," or "I'm incompetent." Therefore, the strategy of taking control is a way to compensate for the doubt.

Bill works at a restaurant. Although he is rubbed the wrong way by a couple he is waiting on, he provides them top-notch service, even giving them extra care and attention. They pay for their meal by credit card and leave him the receipt with no tip. Feeling victimized, Bill's powerless doubt is activated, and his desire is to take control of the situation by running after the customers and yelling a sarcastic comment. As it did to Bill, doubt can sometimes lead us to choose a poor behavioral option.

The acts of choosing to avoid a necessary task, quitting without trying, demanding complete control, pleasing others at the expense of yourself, defending yourself, delegating when it would be more logical for you to do it, turning off and shutting down when action is necessary, becoming a perfectionist when perfection is not necessary, and worrying rather than taking action are driven by doubt. The link between your behavioral choice and doubt is the if/then rule that develops. The more self-doubt you experience, the more rigid the rule. This leads to using a behavioral strategy that is not the best fit for a given situation. Over time, the rules lead to fewer and fewer choices of actions.

By the end of this chapter, you will be armed with confidence and you will know that either you can handle the situation (competence) or you will be likable regardless of what you do (desirable), thus you'll be more likely to problem solve and follow a plan of action.

The If/Then Messages

Ever wonder where your choices of behavior come from? They come from doubt. Doubt leads to fear, which inhibits your actions. If/then messages are the intrinsic rules you make that connect doubt to your behavior. You believe your if/then rules help you navigate life. Sometimes if/then rules do help you, but often they actually interfere with your goals. If/then rules are a problem when they lead you to choose a behavioral strategy that does not work or is harmful. Typically, if/then rules that are driven by doubt are followed *all* the time in *all* situations, whether they make sense under current circumstances or not. Confidence brings the freedom and the ability to break the if/then rules.

Jane exemplifies how doubt shapes behavior. She is a single woman in her mid-twenties and in her second year of teaching at a small parochial school. Jane wants everyone to like her. It's been that way her whole life. Lacking confidence, Jane worries about what everybody else thinks of her. She hears rumors going around school that she takes advantage of her colleagues. She automatically wants to defend herself. Defending herself is her old pattern, and something she tells us she is actively trying to stop because she believes it only makes things worse for her. Instead, she tries to sit back and bite her tongue, reminding herself what kind of person she is and that she need not worry what anyone else thinks. Instead of following the rule "If people say bad things about me, then I have to defend myself or they won't like me" she has begun to live by this healthier rule: "If people say bad things about me, then ignore it because I already know I am likable regardless of their opinion." Recognizing doubt and the role it plays in shaping our rules and driving our behaviors give us the knowledge we need to rewrite our rules and change our behaviors.

How Do If/Then Rules Develop?

Like self-doubt labels, if/then rules develop early in life as a result of internal and external factors. If/then rules often become fixed before an opportunity to test out a different rule becomes possible. Think of Jennifer, a young girl playing at a friend's house. The friend asks if she would prefer to watch a movie or jump on the trampoline. Jennifer tells her friend she does not care, and they begin to watch the movie. But Jennifer finds the movie boring and tells her friend assertively that she has changed her mind and now wants to go jump on the trampoline. The friend does not want to stop watching the movie and tells Jennifer to go out on the trampoline by herself. Jennifer already doubts her desirability and is likely to think, "My friend does not like me enough to join me outside on the trampoline." This rule then develops: "If I had acquiesced and not asserted myself, then my friend would like me. If I assert myself, then I will be rejected." Once we start to live by our rules, we get stuck in the habit of following them whether they make sense or not. In this case, Jennifer may grow into an adult who fails to ever assert herself, always fearing rejection. The rule becomes a life pattern.

The more rigid your rules, the more self-doubt you carry with you. If Jennifer had realized she was likable whether she asserted herself or not, she would have been freer to state her desires and thus would have realized her rule need not be rigidly true. In comparison, the person who doubts her competence often relies on perfectionism as her strategy of choice: "If I make a mistake, then I am a failure. If I do it perfectly, then I am a success." If you can learn to accept, you can be a success even if you are not perfect and even if you fail in a specific situation. In this way the rigid rules disintegrate. The goal is to recognize the rules are made-up assumptions designed to protect you. Unfortunately, instead of protecting you, the rules put you on a path to harm.

The Development of Internal If/Then Rules

Let's look at possible experiences in which internal if/then rules can develop. These experiences can be anything that leaves a lasting impression on you. They can be significant or big events in our life or seemingly trivial situations. Some examples of a significant event are divorce of parents, abuse, neglect, moving, favoritism in the household, difficulties with friends, being picked on or teased, struggling with schoolwork, and having a critical coach.

Here are some rules one might develop in response to a divorce: "If I had been loved, then they would have stayed together"; "if I had been good, then they would have stayed together, so if I am lovable, people won't leave me"; or "if I am good, people will love me." Abuse might lead one to think: "If I am abused, then I am bad." Neglect may cause a rule such as this one: "If I go out of my way to please others, then I won't be neglected." Moving could arouse this rule: "If I get attached, then I will be hurt, but if I avoid intimacy, then I won't get hurt."

A seemingly trivial comment or action by someone may cause you to question yourself. For example, someone says you smell bad, and you spend the rest of your life worried that you actually do emit an odor.

A rule can also be the result of a significant situation or be caused by something you heard or read in the media that had a tremendous effect on you. An example of this is thinking back to 9/11 terrorist attacks. Most of us can remember exactly where we were when we heard about the first plane crashing into the first World Trade Center. Can you remember being glued to your television, computer, or radio and being worried about what was going to happen next? You may have developed one of these rules: "If I go out to crowded places or travel, then I am vulnerable to harm," but "If I stay home or stay away from popular places and don't travel, then I won't be vulnerable to harm."

IDENTIFY WHERE YOUR INTERNAL RULES CAME FROM

Take out a piece of paper and write down the childhood, adolescent, and adulthood experiences that have had a major effect on you. Next to each experience, write down the rules that you may have developed from it. Here are some examples:

Experience: Jake struggled to get good grades in math. His parents appeared irritated that they needed to spend extra time helping him. Rather than ask anyone for help, Jake spends an excessive amount of time trying to teach himself the course materials and doing his homework.

Internal Rules That Developed: "If I do my work perfectly, then people won't find out I'm not smart." "If I make mistakes, then people will find out that I am not smart." "If I don't struggle in school, then I am smart." "If I struggle in school, then I am not smart."

Experience: Sarah's friends get invited to a mutual friend's slumber party, and she is not invited. Another friend tells her she is not invited to sleep over because the girl was allowed to invite only two friends, and Sarah would have made three.

Internal Rules That Developed: "If I am included, then I am liked." "If I am not included, then I am not liked."

Notice the *then* in the if/then rules is what the event *means* to the person who developed the rule. It's about what the person did or did not do or what others did or did not do. This meaning is the doubt label.

Now, try it yourself:

Experience:

Internal Rules That Developed:

The Development of External If/Then Rules

External rules are those that the outside world has placed on us rather than the rules that we place on ourselves. Stop and think for a moment about the rules you have in your life. Can you go through a typical day without being aware of any of the external rules that affect what you do? As children, our parents and other adults make and enforce rules. Rules can be as simple as this: "If your work is all done, then you can play." Or they can be complex: "If you talk back to someone, then you are a bad child." The media pushes rules on us all the time. "If you use our product, then you will find love"; "If you drive this car, then the world will notice you"; "If you demand your rights, you won't be taken advantage of"; "If you are thin, then the world will love you"; "If you are overweight, then the world will reject you"; "If you go to college, then you will get a good job"; "If you work hard all the time, then you will be successful"; "If you focus on yourself, then you are selfish."

Do these rules work? How powerful was the person or organization that preached them? How susceptible were you? Now stop and think about the rules you have had throughout your life—in school, at work, on the roadway, in past relationships, from the media, and in your current home. Did those rules come from the outside world or did they come from within you?

How many of those external rules were spelled out? Or did you make the link? Some rules are explicitly expressed, whereas others are implied—for example, your brother gets more attention because he has better grades; a coach tells you repeatedly that even if you try your best, you still won't be good enough to be a starter; a significant other tells you that if you have a disagreement, then the relationship is over. Based on your own experiences and observations your personal if/then rules begin to develop: "If I am perfect like my brother, then I will get attention or love"; "If I try, then I will fail anyway, so why try"; or "If I assert myself and disagree, then I will be rejected."

IDENTIFY WHERE YOUR EXTERNAL RULES CAME FROM

Take out a piece of paper and write down the childhood, adolescent, and adulthood experiences that taught you about the world around you. Next to each experience, write down the rules that may have developed from it. Here are some examples:

Experience: Pete sees that the people around him get noticed and are popular because of their clothes, cars, and homes. He overspends on his credit cards and avoids coming up with a realistic budget.

External Rules That Developed: "If I look successful, then people think I'm desirable." "If I don't look successful, then people will not find me desirable."

Experience: Amy notices that some women in her firm make partner. She copies them and begins to spend countless hours at work, trying to take control of every case and refusing to delegate to associates.

External Rules That Developed: "If I control everything, then they will think I'm competent." "If I delegate, then people will think I'm incompetent."

Be aware that the *then* in the if/then rules can develop from explicit or implicit rules from the outside world. Explicit rules are direct messages you receive from significant others, family, friends, teachers, coaches, and the media. Implicit rules develop from your interpretation of personal experiences or observations of others in the world. The meaning you derive from these observations guides the development of the if/then rule, which in turn leads us to fuel our doubt label.

Now, try it yourself:

Experience:
External Rules That Developed:

Positive and Negative If/Then Messages

People develop both positive and negative if/then messages. The positive if/then messages help stop doubt from being activated. Positive rules set up expectations that if we do a specific behavioral strategy, the result will be favorable. For example, if Jessica does not assert herself, then she will be loved. Negative rules, on the other hand, tell us if we choose a certain behavioral strategy, a negative result will follow and our doubt will be activated. For example, if Jessica asserts her opinion, then she will not be loved. Identifying both your positive and negative if/then messages helps you understand the behavioral strategies you chose. Rigidly following your rules takes away your ability to choose from multiple options. Understanding the ineffectiveness of your rules frees you to break them and choose other effective courses of action.

Can You Relate to Sam?

Sam sits at his desk late in the day on a sunny Friday afternoon. Everyone else has left the office leaving him to wonder why he is still there missing the golf game he would have rather been playing. He is dwelling on the fact that his accountant has given him unsolicited advice on how to manage his employees. In addition, his brother has told him how to handle a difficult situation with his son. He feels as if the world were looking at him through a critical lens, and he is not measuring up. Sam has chosen to stay late doing work that could have waited so he can prove to others that he can do more and get more results than any of his employees. However, no one seems to notice or acknowledge the extra work he does or the results that he gets. The old pattern of pushing hard to prove to others that he is a success continues and leads him to compromise his plans and suffer. Furthermore, dwelling on his accountant's and brother's advice leads him to believe others doubt his competence and question his success, which leads him to doubt himself.

Although intellectually he knows that he is competent and a success, emotionally he still feels the failure. Instead of leaving the office, his internal rules tell him to keep working. His internal rules and family messages tell him: "If I work harder and longer than everyone else, then people will see how capable and competent I am"; "If I deliver more than anyone else, then I am a success"; "If I deliver less than exceptional results, then I failed"; "If people praise my success, then I am a success"; "If people fail to recognize or praise my success, then I am incompetent;" "If people give me advice, then I am incompetent"; "If people trust me to do things the way I want, then I am competent and a success." Although Sam tries to follow his rules—working late, doing extra work, and taking charge—he still feels inadequate. No amount of work or success ever gets him the acknowledgment and the kudos he is seeking. Instead, he hears the unsolicited advice as criticism of his competence and negation of his success.

Can You Relate to Jill?

Jill sits at her desk wondering why her mother doesn't seem to recognize that she is a good daughter. Jill keeps replaying the anniversary party she threw the night before for her parents. As she mingled with family members and her parents' friends, she heard many compliments on the party, but none directly credited her. Although Jill organized and arranged every detail of the party as well as paid the lion's share of the costs, her parents' toasted the room and never thanked or acknowledged her efforts. In fact, her parents had all their daughters stand up with their significant others, except for Jill who stood up alone, and talked about how there is nothing more important to them than the joys of their grandchildren. After that, Jill sat down and let her sisters and their children take center stage. At the end of the party, she quietly paid the bill and waited to drive her parents home. Her siblings made excuses not only for why they couldn't contribute more to the party but also for why they couldn't chauffeur their parents. The old pattern repeated itself: Jill continued to acquiesce and felt shortchanged in the process.

Believing she did not do a good enough job to be praised, the doubt label of not being lovable flashed in neon, and Jill's mood and energy level sunk. Her internal rules and family messages said: "If I am perfect enough and please others, they will love me"; "If I am acknowledged and taken care of, I am loved"; "If I am taken advantage of, I deserved it and am unloved"; "If I am flawed, others will not love me." Although Jill followed her own rules—trying to be perfect, saying yes to every request, and trying her best to please everyone—the acknowledgment and love never came. The positive if/then messages help stop the doubt label of being unlovable from being activated. If Jill is perfect, then she believes she will be loved. On the other hand, if Jill is not perfect, she will not be loved. Although Jill compensated by trying to please everyone, not asserting herself with her siblings and compromising her own needs for the needs of others, doubt led her to draw the conclusion that she is not good enough to be loved.

IDENTIFYING YOUR POSITIVE AND NEGATIVE IF/THEN MESSAGES

Think back to the most recent stressful situation you faced and identify your behavior. Did it reflect your typical response or was it atypical? Write down the following information.

1. My behavioral strategy or strategies:

   • _____

   • _____

   • _____

   • _____

2. My positive if/then statement:

   • If I _____ [your behavioral strategy],

   • then _____ [your doubt label that won't get activated].

3. My negative if/then statement:

• If I _____ [your behavioral strategy],

• then _____ [your doubt label that gets activated].

4. People often have many paired positive and negative if/then statements they live by. Record as many as you can think of:

• Positive: If _____ ,
  then _____ .

• Negative: If _____ ,
  then _____ .

• Positive: If _____ ,
  then _____ .

• Negative: If _____ ,
  then _____ .

Having trouble? Here are some examples:

POSITIVE IF/THEN MESSAGES	NEGATIVE IF/THEN MESSAGES
If I am perfect, then I am a success.	If I make a mistake, then I am a failure.
If I am perfect, then I will be liked.	If I am not perfect, then I won't be liked.
If I always say yes, then I won't be rejected.	If I assert myself, then I will be rejected.
If I constantly delegate, then I'll succeed.	If I do it alone, then I'll fail.
If I am in control, then I have power.	If I am taken advantage of, then I am powerless.

How If/Then Messages Operate in Different Areas of Your Life

Although our rules are generalized across our life situations, they become more likely to be followed under duress. Think back to the major domain of your self-doubt. The person who cares most about being competent will have more rigid rules in areas of performance and achievement. The person who cares most about being loved or being a good person will have more rigid rules in interpersonal areas.

Performance Situations

Performance situations, whether it is in the classroom, the workplace, the athletic field, the knitting club, the book club, the board meeting, or entertaining at home, will activate rules in competency-driven individuals who are burdened with self-doubt. The positive if/then rule can take the form of "If I do more than what is expected, then I will be viewed as competent." The negative if/then rule can then develop as "If I do only what is expected, then I will be viewed as incompetent." Striving to always deliver extra creates unnecessary stress, and failing to meet one's expectations will guarantee fuel for more self-doubt.

Tom, a financial adviser and asset manager, yielded his customers a lower profit this year than any other year in his thirty-five years on the job. His customers were no worse off than the rest of the population, but he judged himself a failure because he could not live up to his positive rule that says, "If I do exceptionally well, then I am competent." Instead his negative rule, "If I perform only at an average level, then I am incompetent," fueled his self-doubt.

Social Situations

Social situations, like dates, social outings, vacation travel, holiday and special-occasion parties, phone conversations, and email and text messages, will activate rigid adherence to the rules in the person who cares about being liked or being a good person. They are more likely to be concerned about wearing the right clothes, writing the email properly, or saying the right thing. The positive if/then rule may be "If I do what they ask, then they will like me or I will be a good person" or "If I say the right thing, then they will like me." This negative if/then rule may then follow: "If I don't do what they ask, then they won't like me or I won't be a good person" or "If I don't dress appropriately, then they will see what a loser I am." Needing to please others and fearing rejection lead the socially oriented person to often ignore his or her own needs in consideration for others, which often leads to disappointment and sadness.

Think of Jill's constant doubt leading her to question if she is a good person and if she is lovable. Her positive and negative rules lead her to crumble emotionally at the first sign of criticism or when actions don't take her needs into consideration.

Take the example of Jill's last boyfriend forgetting that he spent his last birthday with her. Jill had gone out of her way to buy him a plethora of gifts and to travel a long distance to see him. She feels completely rejected by his lack of memory. In addition, although she repeatedly asks him to not make fun of her quirky habits, he teases her. Jill believes the only reason he continues to hurt her feelings even when she asks him not to, is because she is unworthy of love. Jill's response at first is to give more and try harder. Failing to receive the love and adoration she is looking for, she begins to distance herself from the relationship, and it fails.

Rule Replacement: Giving Up the Rules

Now that you know your rules, it is time to experiment with giving them up. Instead of throwing your rules away entirely, follow them only in the situations in which they make sense. Sometimes it is better to remain quiet and not assert yourself, and sometimes it is better to do a good job rather than to do more than what was expected. The key is to make your rules less rigid.

Testing Your Rules

The best way to test a rule is to break it and examine the consequences. Did your predictions come true or were data provided that contradicted your prediction? Consider the rule "If I assert myself, then I will be rejected." Choosing to never assert yourself and to be passively submissive to the needs of others may have led to social acceptance. However, that social acceptance is most likely a result of a multitude of factors and not simply the result of yielding to others. Social acceptance often comes from being genuine, honest, reliable, fun, interesting, smart, or funny or from just being there for someone. Asserting oneself need not even play a role. To find out if asserting yourself is as dangerous as you are making it out to be, you must break the rule and assess the consequences. Instead of agreeing to the restaurant your spouse, friend, employer, or relative chooses, you can pick one you prefer. Instead of watching a movie you are not interested in, you can speak up and ask to see the one you want. Instead of passively letting the other person have first pick, you can state your preference. Breaking your rules in this way opens the door to freedom. Fortunately, your rules get tested all the time, even when you are not the one testing them.

Think of all the people in your life and in the media who do not follow your rules. They have run the experiment for you. Consider all the brides who assertively took control of their wedding arrangements and how few of them were rejected. Think of all the people who asserted themselves with you and yet you did not reject them. Any rule can be examined by looking outside of yourself and at the world at large. The bottom line is that no rule fits all the time because there are no absolutes in the real world.

RULE REPLACEMENT EXERCISE

Design an experiment so you can begin to rewrite your rules.

1. Plan the experiment. If you care most about being competent, choose an experiment in the performance/achievement area. Pick one of your if/then rules to test—for example: "If I make a mistake, then I am a failure." If you care most about being considered desirable (loved, liked, or being a good person) choose an experiment in the interpersonal/social areas. Pick one of your if/then rules to test—for example: "If I always say yes, then people will like me."

2. Do the experiment. For example: make a mistake at work, don't return a phone call, skip an errand, arrive somewhere several minutes late, don't double-check your work, miss a ball, don't ask how someone is, don't offer to do a favor, say no, cancel a social plan, or arrive at a function several minutes late.

3. Collect the data. How did your if/then prediction compare to the actual outcome? Write it down:

• _____

• _____

• _____

• _____

• _____

Confidence-Building Rules

Now, it's time to develop your confidence-building rules. Confidence-building rules are adaptive, flexible rules based on believing in yourself. They come from recognizing you are both competent and desirable. Confidence-building rules arm you so that you no longer have to compensate for doubt. They enable you to be free to choose a behavior that makes sense in any given situation. Instead of choosing avoid, quit, control, please, defend, delegate, distract, perfection, or worry, you can choose a strategy that is in your best interest. The competent and desirable person does not need rigid rules to prove he or she is competent or desirable. Such a person is free to make mistakes, ask for help, take on difficult tasks, delegate when necessary, be assertive, take care of his or her own needs, develop realistic expectations, and use good problem-solving strategies.

Now it is time to write your new confidence-building rules. Here are some examples to get you started:

I am competent, so I do not have to be perfect.

I am competent, so I can make mistakes without fear.

I am competent, so I can miss out on some sleep and still function.

I am desirable, so I don't have to be perfect.

I am desirable, so it is okay to say no.

I am desirable, so I can take care of my needs too.

Write down your new confidence-building rules:

- _____
- _____
- _____
- _____
- _____

The Bottom Line

Rigid rules come from self-doubt about your competency or your desirability or both. Self-confidence that you are competent and desirable frees you from those rules. Breaking your rules is the only way to test that you no longer need to let the rules get in your way.

Chapter Six

Living Without Doubt

Now it is time to start living without doubt. Free of the bias of doubt, you can be confident throughout the day. At this point, you can recognize doubt is just a false, interfering barrier that gets in your way. You can now easily knock down this barrier with the skills of identifying and labeling doubt, questioning it with facts, and rethinking it. Once the barrier is removed, doubt evaporates and confidence takes over. By squashing doubt, you become liberated and a new view of yourself is strengthened.

Why is confidence so important? For one, without confidence, every situation you face appears dangerous. The perception of threat activates your internal alarm system, adding stress to your already taxed system. The danger is the fear that you cannot handle a situation or the fear that you are being negatively judged in some way. Also, without confidence, you often fail to recognize your own assets and strengths.

By effectively removing doubt, this allows confidence to strengthen and grow. Confidence now has the advantage of deactivating our unnecessary alarms. By recognizing that we can handle situations and not fear other peoples' judgments, our world is safe. Our greatest resource is confidence, and carrying it with us at all times is our ticket to success.

Developing Your Confidence Belief

What have you been calling yourself? What is the doubt label that has plagued you? Now name it. Is it still 100 percent accurate? The answer is it is not 100 percent true, 100 percent of the time. Now it is time to figure out your new label—your confidence belief. Your confidence belief is based on a more realistic, accurate, and balanced appraisal of the doubt label. What is it that you would like to say about yourself? What have you heard others say about you? Let's figure it out together.

Can You Relate to Sam?
Sam finally understands that he does measure up. He has learned to apply his smarts to himself, and he can now see his own positive capital and lack of deficits as clearly as if they were numbers on a spread sheet. Working in the black, he no longer needs anyone to validate his success. Sam can list his assets: smart, superb businessman, financially successful, socially skilled, savvy, and able to carry a large load of responsibilities simultaneously. The fact that he is the go-to person whenever there are business crises speaks to his competence. He now recognizes that people solicit his advice, which serves as additional support for his competence.

Can You Relate to Jill?
Jill has learned that the doubt label of being unlovable feels true but is not a fact. The facts support a very different view. Objectively,

she has come to understand that she is in fact lovable, desirable, and worthy. Jill is good enough and, more important is lovable, regardless of what her feelings tell her. Forcing herself to see the evidence, she learns that people often compliment her attractiveness, sense of style, cooking skills, decorating, kindness, generosity, graciousness, and compassion. Jill is now able to see that she is a particularly good daughter, sister, aunt, girlfriend, and friend and gets additional confirmation from those around her. Furthermore, when anyone needs someone to talk to or confide in, she is always the person they choose. Focusing on the facts, Jill now appreciates her own attractiveness, desirability, and goodness to others. And now she can say, "I am lovable."

Building Your Confidence Belief

Now it's time to put a name to your new confidence belief. Use the table below to help you find your possible beliefs. First, see if you can find your doubt label or some derivation of it. Next, replace it with your new confidence belief. You could use one or more of the terms in the table or you may create one that seems right for you. This new belief is the new beginning to the new, confident you. What would it be like to hear yourself saying one of the confidence beliefs listed in the table?

OLD DOUBT LABELS	POTENTIAL CONFIDENCE BELIEFS
I'm stupid.	I'm smart. I'm not stupid. I'm better than average. I'm street smart. I'm clever. I'm sharp. I'm quick.
I'm not good enough.	I'm good enough. I'm better than average. I'm good.

I'm weak.	I'm strong. I'm not weak. I'm powerful. I'm durable. I'm resilient. I'm tough. I'm solid.
I'm inadequate.	I'm adequate. I'm competent. I'm capable. I'm sufficient. I'm acceptable. I'm qualified.
I'm a failure.	I'm a success. I'm not a failure. I'm accomplished. I'm a winner.
I'm not good enough.	I do measure up. I'm good enough. I'm worthy. I'm first rate. I'm good quality.
I'm unlikable.	I'm likable. I'm desirable.
I'm unattractive.	I'm attractive. I'm a desirable package.
I'm bad.	I'm good. I'm decent. I'm respectable. I'm worthwhile.
I'm boring.	I'm not boring. I'm appealing. I'm interesting.
I'm unlovable.	I'm lovable. I'm cared about. I matter.

REALITY CHECK EXERCISE

1. Write down your old doubt label:

Examples: I'm not good enough. I'm unattractive.

• _____

2. Write down your confidence belief:

Examples: I am good enough. I am a desirable package.

• _____

Strategies for Collecting Data for Your New Confidence Belief

Now that you have your confident belief, it is time to confirm your confidence and collect data in support of it!

You can collect data about doubt in the area of competency by one or more these methods:

- Objectively evaluate your performance at work or at a recreational activity and record the facts (verbal feedback, written feedback, bonuses, job security, responsibilities given to you, longevity of employment, title, solicitation of your knowledge, advice, feedback).

- Ask for feedback if you don't have the information.

- Interview a friend, relative, or colleague.

- Think of yourself as a job applicant and pretend to evaluate yourself for a job in the workforce or in the home.

- Ask yourself if there have been complaints, reprimands, or grievances filed against you.

- Ask yourself what responsibilities you manage and take care of in your daily life.

- Ask yourself if you have handled any stressors, problems, or difficult tasks currently or in your past.

- Ask yourself if you manage to juggle lots of things.

You can collect data about doubt in the area of desirability by one or more of these methods:

- Ask yourself if you have any plans with friends or have had any invitations in the past or recently.

- Ask yourself if anyone has called, texted, or emailed you.

- Ask yourself if someone has smiled or greeted you.

- Ask yourself if you have called family members, friends, or colleagues and recall their reaction.

- Look at yourself in the mirror and identify your physical attributes, such as your hair, height, smile, teeth, eyes, complexion, nails, or specific body part.

- Ask yourself if anyone has given you a compliment.

- Ask yourself if you have any special qualities, such as humor, conversational skills, talent, or a vibrant personality.

- Ask yourself if you are reliable, responsible, considerate, kind, generous, thoughtful, or caring.

Write down the data in support of your new confidence belief(s):

- _____

- _____

- _____

- _____

- _____

Expand Your Confidence

To continue to build your confidence belief, it is important to appreciate the pieces that make you whole and learn to stop focusing on any one part. *You are a package, not any single item.* Expand your self-definition by increasing your awareness of characteristics that define you. Each of us is composed of a multitude of qualities that make us unique. The problem is that doubt causes us to take a magnifying glass to one specific feature rather than looking at all the assets that make you whole.

COMMODITY EXERCISE

Let's try an exercise: Imagine you are a commodity, and you need to sell yourself on the open market. What do you have to sell? Make a list of your assets:

1.

2.

3.

4.

5.

6.

7.

8.

9.

10.

Need some help? Here are some questions to help expand your list. Is your **brain** a commodity? Are you book smart, street smart, life smart, or all of the above? Do you excel in school or are you the one who can get most of the questions right in *Jeopardy*? Do you know how to make things happen, elicit the cooperation of others, tackle problems or work the crowd? Do you know when to follow the rules and when to bend them? Do you know the difference between the important and unimportant goals? Everyone has some smarts. It is time to give yourself credit for your smarts. Now add the applicable characteristics to your list of assets.

Do you appreciate your **physical** assets? Physical appearance is a complex combination of individual pieces. Instead of judging yourself on any one attribute, like your weight or your nose, look at all the facets of your appearance that are positive. When you examine your physical appearance through an objective lens, which personal assets begin to come into view? Do you like your smile, your teeth, your eyes or your bone structure? How about your skin color, hair color, hands, nails, feet, or another body part? What do people tend to compliment you on? You will be able to find lots of things to put on your asset list if you accept that there are things that you can like about your appearance even if there are things you don't like. Add these items to your list.

How about your **personality**? Are you funny or do you have a good sense of humor? Are you laid back? Are you caring, thoughtful, compassionate, reliable, conscientious, helpful, trustworthy, or loyal? Do you know how to listen or are you a great conversationalist? What about your role with others? Are you a good parent, sibling, family member, friend, colleague, committee member, neighbor, or person in general? Add each applicable quality to your list.

What **other strengths** do you have that you are failing to recognize? Are you creative, hardworking, athletic, organized, neat, put together, or musical? Are you good with money, are you an animal lover, or are you fun? Do you have interests, such as music, art, cooking, sports, wine, theater, movies, or reading? Add these assets to your list.

Now look at the list and see the assets that distinguish you. See that you are a positive, complex commodity.

Your list is a list of facts, not feelings. Facts are the objective, reliable view of yourself that builds and strengthens your confidence. Feelings are the subjective, unreliable view of you that strengthens the grip of self-doubt. When you use your feelings as your sole guide, you compromise the truth. Remember it is always good to check out the facts by looking at the situation objectively or by collecting feedback from others.

Changing and Chipping Away at Doubt

Doubt is fueled by your doubt distortions. Rather than looking at the world through an objective clear lens, you see everything through the dark-tinted lens of doubt. For example, a person with an incompetency doubt label uses her working late into the night and on weekends as evidence. The real deal, or the more accurate conclusion, is that the job dictates more work than time allows and most of her colleagues are working there right along with her. In fact, one employee who has not been putting in the time is likely to be fired. Actually, the facts are she is doing a good job and has received regular bonuses and positive evaluations each year.

The person whose doubt label is "I'm not valued," feels this when he flies into town to attend an important social function, and his best friend texts him that he is too busy to pick him up at the airport but may be able to spend time with him much later in the afternoon. But then he is able to remember that his friend chose him to be the best man at his wedding and calls him regularly and that his wife left him because he was too busy for her. By reviewing the facts, he knows that his friend is actually overcommitted, always adding one more obligation to an already unreasonable schedule.

Now it is time for you to remove your doubt bias by teaching yourself to look at the world more accurately. Instead of paying attention to and focusing on only the fuel for our doubt, learn to recognize and be aware of all the information that contradicts doubt and builds confidence.

The Snapshot

For the new confidence belief to take hold, it is important that you not trip yourself up by using isolated events to deconstruct it. Most of us do not realize that we tend to focus on a specific or a series of specific moments in time to define who we are as a person. Focusing on those moments leads to broad, inaccurate conclusions of doubt. Instead, focusing on the summation of many moments leads to a more valid and a more confident view. The goal is to help you look at yourself through the lens of confidence rather than through the lens of those magnified moments of doubt.

Can You Relate to Liz?

Liz is a divorced woman in her forties with two children, and she has an MBA from a prestigious business school. She has successfully worked her way up the corporate ladder into a coveted vice president position at a Fortune 500 company. After the quarterly report comes out, she recognizes the company solvency is in question. Later that day, she is informed that the company may be sold, and everyone's job security is in jeopardy. Believing she will be one of the first ones on the chopping block, her old doubt of failure surfaces.

Sitting at her desk, Liz places her head down and thinks about specific moments from her past that confirm failure. As the slide show in her mind begins, she reviews the sharp downward turn of her stocks from the news this morning. Her thoughts then turn to her last job. Four years ago she was working for a much smaller company with solid job security, but was doing work she did not particularly enjoy. Now, she reviews her decision and thinks what a failure she was to leave such a good situation. She then flashes onto college where she remembers dreading not being able to get a job because of what she believed were mediocre credentials. Looking back on her classes, she remembers always having to work harder and longer than everyone else, which leads her to question her ability to succeed. Of course, this always brings back the memories of not being asked to the prom, not being elected class treasurer, and the father who constantly criticized her. The picture in her mind goes as far back as elementary school and the shame of forgetting her homework and needing to be pulled out of class for reading support. These earliest memories are linked to the development of failure doubt.

Of course, it makes sense that Liz is experiencing distress at this moment. Especially because she is reviewing her life through limited snapshots of time; it is understandable, but inaccurate, for her to think of herself as a failure. Now let's replay Liz's past through an unbiased, broader lens. Here is a more realistic way to look at what happened:

Snapshot: Downward Turn of Stocks

Real Deal: The entire market has taken a downward turn and has nothing to do with which stocks she chose or for that matter anything to do with her personally. Despite the downward turn, her portfolio is diversified, her mortgage is reasonable, and her car is paid off. Her financial picture is solid.

Snapshot: Leaving Her Old Job

Real Deal: At the time, the long list of advantages of her new job outweighed any potential price in leaving. Four years of gain (vice president, more money, more prestige, better benefits, and lots of perks) have confirmed that decision.

Snapshot: College, Mediocre Credentials, She Works Harder and Longer Than Others

Real Deal: In reality, plenty of people worked hard and long. It was true that some people seem to get results with very little effort, but others worked hard and long and still could not cut it. The fact is that Liz was at a top-notch school, and her degree alone can open doors. Everyone was loaded down with senior projects and classroom work; no one had time to pursue extra-curricular activities.

Snapshot: No Date for the Prom

Real Deal: Lots of kids, including some of Liz's friends, stayed home that night. In fact, a group of them, including Liz, wound up going to the shore and having a great time. The fact is Liz could have had a date to the prom but declined an offer from a young man she was not interested in.

Snapshot: Not Elected Class Treasurer

Real Deal: There were 600 kids in her high school senior class. That means that 598 other kids were also not elected treasurer. The person who did win was more popular but not necessarily more qualified.

Snapshot: Dad Was Critical

Real Deal: Dad was critical with everybody all the time. In fact, he had a hard time keeping employees because he was insulting. Although Dad was hard on her, he took the time to drive her to school many mornings and praised her accomplishments.

Snapshot: Forgetting Homework in Elementary School

Real Deal: Plenty of kids forget their homework. It seemed worse for Liz because her mother always made her suffer the consequences. In fact, if Liz realized she had her forgotten homework when her mother was driving, her mom would neither turn around nor agree to bring it to school later.

Snapshot: Needing Reading Support

Real Deal: Several kids in her class, including the so-called smart kids, were in reading support. Looking back on it now, two of her friends in reading support are two of the most successful people she knows. Her father, involved in his work, did not make any time to read with her. Mom had a relaxed attitude, believing that all kids eventually read and that it was the school's job to make that happen.

Snapshot: Job in Perceived Jeopardy

Real Deal: The reality is Liz's job may very well be in jeopardy, but that is a reflection of the economic environment and the shortcomings of her company rather than of her personally. Liz is an expert in her field, is driven, and gets results. This makes her a good commodity in the market. At present, no one has contacted her to indicate that her job is on the line. Even if her division is cut, there are other places in the organization where she would be a good fit.

The bottom line is Liz's failure doubt is causing her to suffer needlessly. Riddled with doubt, she draws conclusions from several isolated moments as confirmation of her doubt label of failure. Reviewing her data through an objective and nondistorted lens leads her to conclude her self-doubt has no merit.

The facts suggest that Liz is a competent, capable, and successful woman. Acknowledging she has had missed opportunities, mess-ups, struggles, and disappointments only shows she is human and *not* that she's a failure. Liz's overall picture clearly shows that whether or not she loses her job, regardless of her past struggles, and disappointing moments, she is not a failure. A more accurate, new confidence belief now reigns and tells her she is successful, has always been successful, and will remain successful, regardless of what happens in the external world.

DOUBT DEBATER EXERCISE

It's time to take the next step yourself. Instead of blindly accepting information as confirmation of your self-doubt label, you can learn to reevaluate that information and rethink your conclusion. Looking at facts through this more accurate perspective will allow self-doubt to weaken and self-confidence to take over. Let's look at all the information you have been using to convince yourself that your doubt label is true and then reevaluate whether those data actually support your doubt.

1. Name your central doubt label(s):

   • _____

   • _____

2. List the evidence (*the snapshot*) that has convinced you that your doubt label or labels are true. Collect data from a

variety of situations—work, school, recreation, home, sports, friendships, relationships, family outings, travel, hobbies, errands, responsibilities—and activities that activated your old doubt.

• _____

• _____

• _____

• _____

3. Examine each item in the list separately. Use the following questions to determine whether the evidence confirms your doubt label. The critical aspect of this exercise is to find valid alternative meanings for the information you provided so that you can objectively discover that doubt caused you to draw the wrong conclusions. Let's open your mind to more realistic possibilities.

What alternative meaning can this information provide other than support of your doubt?

Is there evidence for the alternative view?

What other meanings would other people give to your data?

Are your conclusions based on feelings or on facts?

If you were on the witness stand, would the facts support the verdict?

Was this particular incident or result a reflection of only one situational moment?

Is your conclusion true across many situations or true only in this specific situation?

Is there a grain of truth to substantiate your doubt (not a twisting of facts) or have you drawn an unfair, sweeping, general conclusion?

Are there situations in which your doubt conclusion would have been exactly the opposite or would not have fit?

Are there valid environmental factors (for example, the economy) beyond your personal actions that contributed to the situation?

Are you the only cause or did someone else play a role? Was he or she the culprit in this situation?

4. Record only the factual data along with your new realistic conclusions (*the real deal*):

   • _____

   • _____

   • _____

   • _____

   • _____

5. Now it is time to recognize the following:

   Your doubt label or labels were not confirmed.

   Your new confidence belief or beliefs are supported.

6. Name your new confidence beliefs:

   • _____

   • _____

7. Give each of your new confidence beliefs the support it needs by reminding yourself of the data that confirmed your new view.

• _____

• _____

• _____

• _____

To see the real deal, remember to look at the whole picture. Recognize that snapshots don't tell the whole story; you need to look at the facts not your feelings. Consider all the possibilities. See the situation through the confidence perspective!

Confidence-Building Cards

Confidence-building cards reinforce the new confidence beliefs you are building. They reiterate the facts you have collected and the healthy conclusions you have drawn. They are free of the doubt distortions and doubt labels. Confidence-building cards are opportunities for you to acknowledge your struggles, disappointments, or short-comings and ascribe new healthier meaning to those events.

It is important to write your confidence beliefs out onto the confidence-building cards. By writing the beliefs on a piece of paper, you can see the undiluted facts. They cannot be twisted, turned, and distorted in your mind to fit the way you feel at a given moment. There is a natural tendency for us as humans to let our emotions color our perceptions. In addition, instead of taking personal responsibility, you can use the cards to help you stay objective. Seeing the facts and valid conclusions on paper allows objectivity to reign.

Don't underestimate the importance of creating cards. Your brain is a powerful instrument, but it needs to be exercised. Reading and rereading your confidence-building cards conditions your brain. Like developing a physical fitness routine for your body, you need to find a way to retrain your brain. The cards can create the desired effect if you follow some of these strategies:

Put them on your night table and read them before you get into and get out of bed.

Put them in your bathroom and look at them as you brush your teeth.

Put them in your wallet or purse and look at them when you're standing in line or waiting for an appointment.

Leave them as voice messages on your cell phone and listen to them whenever you check for other messages.

Leave them as text messages on your cell phone and read them whenever you get a new message.

Put them on your computer as a screen saver.

Program them to display when your scheduler comes up on your computer.

Put them on sticky notes everywhere and anywhere in your house or office.

Put them in your desk drawer so you see them when you reach for a pen.

Put them in your glove compartment and read them at red lights or in car pool lines.

Record them on your MP3 player and listen each time you turn the device on.

Make a schedule and look at them at set times, such as before meals or before you start your car.

For inspiration, consider Liz's confidence-building cards:

I am not a failure!

Although I sometimes feel like a failure and have not always performed as well as I would have liked, I cannot deny my success.

Even if I lose my job, it will not mean I am a failure. Nothing can change the fact that I am already a success.

It is my tendency to focus on my difficulties, which magnifies my perception of failure. It is time to focus on my accomplishments and magnify my success.

Reminding myself of all the hurdles I have jumped (college, rigorous MBA program, and demanding jobs) to cross the finish line supports my success.

I am not only *not* a failure, I am actually a *success!*

Notice that confidence-building cards can remind you of your individual specific accomplishments and social triumphs. They can also be more general summaries and conclusions of confidence. You can find one powerful statement that fortifies your new self view or you can use multiple statements combined. The key is to write only statements that you accept as true. Allowing facts to guide you as you create your confidence cards guarantees a favorable reception.

Try out these confidence-building cards:

I am capable.

I am desirable.

Knowing I am capable and desirable, I can face life fear free!

If you do not believe these three confidence-building statements, it is important that you question the opposing thoughts that continue to feed your doubt. These statements are what you are striving to believe. To help you get there you might try on some of the following confidence-building cards:

I have what it takes to be competent.

I possess the qualities of a desirable person.

I am not helpless.

I am an attractive package.

I have more control or power than I realize.

People do care about me.

I am responsible.

I am a good person.

I am a good problem solver.

I am a loyal and good friend.

The Bottom Line

In this chapter you have effectively squashed doubt and begun to develop and strengthen your confidence beliefs. You have noticed that doubt came from the snapshot, a biased selective picture that magnifies the negatives. Confidence is built on objective, fact-driven logic that cannot be denied. Your brain knows the real deal, and with lots of practice your old feelings will be convinced.

Step 4
Take Action

Take Action

Chapter Seven

Expand Your Confidence

It's time to start living with confidence. As you have learned, your new confidence label is really who you are. Confidence means believing in yourself and your skills. You are a capable and desirable person. It's time to put your confidence into action. Confident, you can live in the moment, fully appreciating your accomplishments and your social life, and effectively coping with your stressors. Picture how much better life is now that you can successfully free yourself from doubt. Notice that your mood is better, you stand up straighter, feel lighter, are less reactive to what others say or do, and are more comfortable in your own skin. Now gain the skills to build your confidence belief and take action as that confident person.

It's time to take a balanced approach to life. When things are going well, you often take for granted how you feel about yourself.

This is the time to pay attention and log in the data to strengthen your confidence belief. However, with life there is stress. When distressing events occur, don't let your confidence be compromised. Learn to acknowledge, accept, and take effective action.

We will now teach you effective skills to face stress with confidence. Are you ready to learn how to tackle life's problems without doubt? It's as easy as the three As: acknowledge, accept, act.

Acknowledge

Acknowledgment is the first step because it allows you to record the facts of the situation. It cues you to view the world through a nonjudgmental lens to accurately identify your emotions, bodily sensations, and external experiences. Free of bias, acknowledging provides the data for acceptance to follow. Here is how you use acknowledgment. All you need to do is pay attention to your emotions, how you physically feel, and what is going on in your world.

Acknowledge Your Feelings
Don't deny your feelings, acknowledge them. This allows you to recognize the reality of the situation. To acknowledge means to identify your feelings. Understand that all feelings are valid and okay. The feelings you experience provide important data. Pay attention to yourself and don't let anyone else tell you how you should feel. No matter what you are feeling, name it. Are you sad, anxious, panicked, fearful, distressed, irritable, frustrated, agitated, hopeless, angry, embarrassed, rejected, lonely, guilty, hurt, afraid, disgusted, insecure, frustrated, ashamed, happy, surprised, excited, relieved, loving, secure, and/or confident?

Acknowledge Your Physical Sensations

Be aware of your bodily sensations. To acknowledge means to identify your bodily sensations. Attend to your body responses without judging them. For example, if your heart is beating fast simply make note of it. Describe the situation without labeling it. Recognize that the sensation does not require deciding if you are having a heart attack, exerting yourself, or experiencing anxiety. It just means specifying the symptom. Pinpoint the physical sensations: aroused, shaky, tired, hungry, drained, tense, nauseous, short of breath, exhausted, revved up, tingly, achy, dizzy, light-headed, foggy, disoriented, tearful, hot, chilled, sweaty, butterflies in the stomach, dry mouth, and/or gastrointestinal distress.

Acknowledge Your External World

Acknowledge means not only admit your feelings and listen to your body but also face the truth of your external world. The key is to acknowledge only the data you observed. It means recognizing real danger or risk and identifying real or potential loss, unpleasantness, hardship, adversity, stress, or annoyance. Here are some examples: Your glasses are lost or broken, your mortgage is due and you don't have the funds, your car broke down and you have no transportation to get to work, your investment portfolio has plummeted, your fiancé has called off the wedding, your teenager is out after curfew, you lost your cell phone, or you have a disagreement with your friend.

Julie's Example of Acknowledgment

Julie's fear is escalating, her body is wound up, and she worries that she has a disaster on her hands. She needs to acknowledge she is anxious and her body is aroused. She should describe the situation that is genuinely causing distress. Julie acknowledges that her child has gotten a speeding ticket and may lose his license if a lesser plea with the judge cannot be negotiated.

David's Example of Acknowledgment

David lives in a constant state of worry and apprehension. His body is tense and his stomach is in knots. He acknowledges that he is scared and physically sick with fear. He has lived modestly his entire life, each year putting a large amount of his income into investments. Checking the financial market news throughout the day he sees evidence that his assets are shrinking. He acknowledges the big picture and sees that the world is in an economic crisis and his assets are worth significantly less.

> **Remember:** *The key is only to acknowledge the information and not to judge it.*

ACKNOWLEDGMENT EXERCISE

Think back to the last time you were distressed. Here is how you can effectively use the acknowledge skill. Write down only the information you observed.

Acknowledge the feelings:
Acknowledge your bodily sensations:
Acknowledge your external world:

Accept

Accepting is the second step in helping your confidence grow. To accept means to draw accurate conclusions based on the factual data and not allow the shadow of doubt to interfere. It allows you to see the situation or event for what it is (acknowledge) and then to draw accurate conclusions (accept). Accepting is only possible when the distorted lens of doubt is removed. To do this, you must look at the situation objectively without judgmental bias. It is the bias that sees hopelessness when it isn't warranted or feels the fear when there is no danger. Don't let uncertainty or doubt lead to derogatory labels of yourself that do not fit. To accept means to recognize that something is not working out the way you would like. Accepting does *not* mean resigning yourself as being your doubt label.

Julie's Example of Acceptance

Julie accepts that there might be negative consequences of her child's speeding ticket, but they are not necessarily as catastrophic as she envisions. Even if there are consequences, she can accept them knowing there are likely solutions to help her handle them. Julie can accept that this might mean he is not ready to have the responsibility of a license or that driving over the speed limit in a twenty-five-mile-per-hour zone is easy to do and not necessarily evidence of irresponsible driving. Julie accepts that his ticket is not a reflection on her. Doubt about herself has no place here because her son's mistake is not a reflection of her character.

David's Example of Acceptance

David accepts that his portfolio shows diminished assets on paper. He recognizes that just because his net value is worth less does not mean that *he* is worth less. The bottom line is the world market is affecting everyone's pocket. It does not diminish his achievements or his success.

Remember: *The key to acceptance is resisting the tendency to make the situation mean something about you personally and thus let your doubt label take over.*

Accept Rather Than Doubt for the Achiever

Performance situations create opportunities for your incompetency doubts to take hold. Obstacles that get in the way of accomplishing simple routines, barriers that block your ability to put solutions into effect, and hindrances that affect daily living all have the potential to activate doubt about being competent. The phone calls that kept you from straightening up the kitchen or returning the emails before you have to run to your appointment mean that you've left a task undone. Do you accept this for what it is? It means only that the task did not get done and things got in your way. Or do you make it mean something personal? For example, do you think, "Because it did not get done, I fell short"? Look at another example: You plan to buy a new cartridge for your printer on the way home from work only to find that the store closed early that day. Do you accept the bad luck of an unfortunate circumstance or do you think that you messed up? Concluding that you messed up is directly linked to doubt and the labeling of yourself as inept, stupid, or incompetent is not far behind. The bottom line is that there is no meaning about you from any of these situations.

Accept Rather Than Doubt Social Interactions

Interpersonal situations create opportunity for your doubts about being desirable to take hold. Complications can get in the way of social commitments, difficulties can put you at odds with other people, and hurdles can get in the way of relationships. All of these obstacles have the potential to activate your doubt about being desirable. One example of a complication is the raging fever of your young child that keeps you from attending your good friend's party. Another example is an aging relative's demands that lead you to cancel a weekend trip with your significant other. Both result in disappointing others. Do you accept your situations as they are or do you conclude you are a bad person for letting others down?

Every time you face a misfortune, obstacle, barrier, or hindrance accept them as the reality of life. Work to make sure you do not make the resulting outcome mean something derogatory about yourself. When you notice you are constructing a negative label about yourself, stop and recognize that doubt has erupted. Replace the exaggerated, negatively biased doubt conclusion with acceptance, and get ready to take action.

Act

Action plays an important role in developing your confidence. Appropriate action means you have not let your doubt label interfere and you are choosing to take logical, helpful steps in accordance with your new confidence beliefs. Instead of engaging in overused strategies (avoid, quit, control, please, defend, delegate, distract, perfection, worry) to feed your doubt, you can choose to take the best possible action. Rather than trying one or several strategies repeatedly across situations you can now choose the best tactic for each specific situation.

Julie's Example of Action
Julie acknowledges her fear, the distress in her body, and the fact that her son got a speeding ticket. She accepts the potential negative consequences and recognizes that it's time to take action. Julie examines her options; after reviewing each one, she decides to

have her son fight the ticket by pleading not guilty. Together they decide to go to court in the hopes of negotiating a lesser offense and thus avoiding the severe penalties that could result from his original ticket. She also decides to make him pay his own fines and to restrict his driving privileges.

David's Example of Action

David acknowledges his apprehension and muscle tension in response to his decreasing net worth. He accepts that his diminished portfolio is not a reflection of his self-worth. His choice of action is to educate himself on world events, watch the market, and take no drastic action at the present time. David knows that he really loses net worth only if he sells precipitously. There is no real loss right now.

Take Appropriate Action

The following tools will help you take successful action. Instead of falling back into old patterns of responding, which may not be the best fit for the situation, it is time to develop healthier habits that lead to finding the best action for each situation.

Power Problem Solving

Effective problem solving means to take action unencumbered by doubt. It allows you to objectively and systematically spell out your options. Doubt permits fear or discouragement to lead you to fail to see options that exist. Confidence opens your eyes to the numerous possibilities. Options can be discovered in multiple ways. You can develop them on your own and by using your resources. These resources can be information gathered from experts, friends, colleagues, relatives, the Internet, books, magazines, and/or newspapers. After you identify several possible options, it is important to list the advantages and disadvantages of each and then to choose the one or ones that seem to be the best fit for the situation in question.

When you look at the advantages and disadvantages, it is important to make sure you are examining valid and objective facts, not doubt-driven, subjective, emotionally colored scenarios. Write down your lists to maximize your ability to see the advantages and disadvantages through an objective lens. Ask yourself if each minus is a real minus or a potential minus? Is the potential minus a real possibility or a statistically unlikely probability? Do the same when examining each plus. Now weigh out the advantages and disadvantages to see which side makes the more compelling choice.

To help with this process, try to visualize using the option(s) you have chosen. You can imagine what that choice looks like from beginning to end as well as what it look likes now and then several weeks, months, or years into the future. If you visualize your choice, you'll be able to realize and address potential problems.

Don't get stuck into thinking there is one perfect option. There are typically lots of good options, and it may be best to think in terms of which options fit better than the others. You can always prioritize your options and start with the first one you have chosen. You can then work your way down the list. You can even change your mind about the option and pick an alternative if the first one does not seem to be working as effectively as you would like.

Once you have made your choice, it is time to make a plan and take action. Set the stage by establishing what you need to do, where and when you plan to do it, and how to make it happen. You can never be too specific. The more details and the clearer the path, the easier it will be to accomplish your plan of action.

Your Steps for Power Problem Solving

1. Identify all the possible options

2. Look at all the advantages and disadvantages of each choice

3. Remember there is no one perfect option. Choose the one or ones that are the best fit given the situation

4. Implement a plan of action

Set Confidence-Based Goals

Did doubt keep you from reaching for goals? Without doubt, the goals you now set can be unlimited. Confidence pushes you to dream, stretch yourself, and to try. Set a new goal for yourself. It can be one that doubt squashed or kept you from considering. It can be something that you always wanted to do but were afraid to try. It can be a goal that you now realize only through your new, confident lens. Remember that your goal can be related to any sphere in life: occupational, social, home, or self-improvement. Here are some examples: apply for a promotion, apply for a new job, start your own business, buy a home, try a new activity, tell a romantic interest how you really feel, start a new friendship.

Going for Your Goal

There are times when working on your goals seems like too much effort or too impossible to reach. Confidence increases motivation, and doubt inhibits motivation. The key is to go for the goal. Success is in the effort and not always in the outcome. Think of all the Olympic athletes who compete. Are the winners only those that return home with medals? Or are the winners all of those talented athletes who made the grade and had the opportunity to compete? Dr. Beck, founder of cognitive therapy, has been twice nominated for the Nobel Prize but has not yet been awarded the honor. How many of us are on that list? Isn't it a mark of his success that he is one of the few scientists to have ever been nominated for that prestigious prize? In a similar manner, your success is in the act of applying for the new job, starting the new business, telling someone how you feel, and trying a new activity.

Make Your Goals Happen

A plan is the specifics to make your goal happen. It is the what, where, when, and how. The more detailed and specific your plan, the easier it will be to follow. Scheduling your plan on a calendar is like making an appointment with your goal, so don't forget to keep it. However, sometimes legitimate obstacles get in the way of our keeping an appointment. For example, sickness, emergencies, and inclement weather. Sometimes excuses are what interfere with your goals. Nonvalid excuses include feeling tired, being low on energy, not feeling like it, watching television, and taking care of nonpressing tasks. Regardless of whether you face legitimate obstacles or nonvalid excuses, the strategy is the same: Reschedule. Rescheduling means writing in another appointment with your goal on your calendar and again trying to keep that appointment. If necessary, reschedule until it happens.

The Truth About Motivation
Motivation is not needed to make things happen. It is the taking of action that increases the motivation. Imagine the alarm clock ringing; do you always feel like getting out of bed? Sometimes you

do not feel like getting up. However, despite your lack of enthusiasm, you can still get out of bed by putting your feet on the floor and starting your day. It is the action that propels us and not the motivation. The reality is you do not have to feel like it to do it. Don't wait for motivation before making changes. Motivation comes from simply taking action.

> To take action, just do it. Get moving, and the motivation will come. You can take action even if you don't feel like it. Don't wait to want to.

Taking the action is the first step in working toward your goal. Having a solid rationale sustains your progress. The rationale, the reason or the advantages of making your goal happen, serve as your intrinsic motivation. For example, on Monday morning you set your alarm clock and got up early to exercise, but by Wednesday you let your comfortable bed get in the way. In addition to continuing to set your alarm clock early and putting action first, you need to get other strategies on board. A good technique is having a list of reasons to continue to exercise. This might help you reach your goal. Your reasons might be weight loss, cardiac health, more energy, or feeling/looking better in your clothes. The longer your list of reasons for reaching your goal, the better this strategy works. The key is to make your list accessible so you can remind yourself of those reasons. Try putting the list of reasons on your computer, PDA, or cell phone or make up a small card that you can keep in your wallet or purse.

Say Good-Bye to Procrastination
Sometimes procrastination can interfere with following through with your goals. Let's figure out if procrastination is an obstacle that gets in *your* way.

ARE YOU A PROCRASTINATOR?

1. Are you the type of person who gets things done or the type who says, "I'll do it later"?

2. Do you tend to make things too complicated?

3. Do you wait for what you want to happen or do you schedule it in?

4. Do you prioritize in a way so that you don't have time to get the important tasks or obligations done?

5. Do you put obstacles in your way so that you can't do it or won't be prepared?

6. Do you wait for help when you really can do it on your own?

7. Do you simply put things off?

8. Do you question your ability and let fear stop you?

SELF-ANALYSIS

If you have answered yes to any of these questions, then procrastination may be interfering with your confidence. It's time to beat procrastination. Are there legitimate skills, information, or help you need before you can take action? If so, acquiring what you need is your first step. If you already have the skills and/or the information necessary to get started, your biggest obstacle may be doubt. Remove the doubt by reminding yourself of the facts. The facts tell you that you're prepared and ready to take action. Beating procrastination entails setting that goal, making that plan, putting action into effect, and reminding yourself of those reasons to work on your goal. Don't let thoughts of doubt be an obstacle to beating procrastination.

Don't Let Your Thoughts Get in the Way of Taking Action

How we think can get in the way of our taking action. The thoughts that get in the way create the problem. We refer to them as *goal-interfering, vanquishing energy* thoughts. Examples of those thoughts are "I'll do it later"; "I don't feel like it"; "It's too hard"; "I don't know where to begin"; "It's too overwhelming"; "I can't handle it"; "What's the point"; and "It's too nice outside to work." If these types of thoughts have crossed your mind, then you might have given up instead of trying to go for it. The give-up thoughts hamper action by fraudulently convincing you to delay. Alternatively, goal-orienting cognitions, or go thoughts, lead us to action. Instead of telling yourself that you'll do it later, tell yourself to do it now. Instead of thinking that you don't know where to begin, tell yourself that if you break the task into small parts, it will be clear where to begin. In place of wondering what the point is, think of the many reasons it makes sense to work on your goal. Remember that the only way you will find out if you should work on your goal is to try and then see what happens. Substituting *go* for *give up* helps you lift the psychological barriers to confidence and success.

Anti-Procrastination Strategy Sheet

GIVE-UP THINKING	GO THINKING
1. I don't feel like doing it.	1. Just by starting, I'll feel better.
2. It's too hard.	2. There's no way to know until I start. Don't assume, just start.

Fill out your own anti-procrastination strategy sheet.

Your Anti-Procrastination Strategy Sheet

GIVE-UP THINKING	GO THINKING
1.	1.
2.	2.

To beat procrastination, set a goal. Write down the reasons you have for reaching your goal. Make a plan for achieving your goal. Then just get started—action doesn't need motivation. Don't give up, go for it!

TO BEAT PROCRASTINATION PLAN

1. Set a goal: _____

2. Reasons for reaching goal:

•_____

•_____

•_____

3. Make a specific plan: _____

4. Take action.

5. Use your go-time thinking.

Give Yourself Credit and You'll Keep Yourself Going

Give yourself the credit you deserve to build confidence and continue to squash doubt. It's time to stop minimizing your accomplishments, telling yourself that anyone could have done it, or that it was no big deal. When you look at what you do, don't make comparisons with your ideal or what you think is the best; don't compare yourself with what you think other people can do. It is important to give yourself credit for the effort and not the outcome. Despite your best efforts, you may not be successful due to factors beyond your control. Giving yourself credit means recognizing your effort as well as your accomplishments.

THE CREDIT BOX: DOCUMENT YOUR DAILY ACHIEVEMENT

Write down at least five things that you can give yourself credit for today.

1.

2.

3.

4.

5.

SELF-ANALYSIS

When giving yourself credit, remember it is the process that counts, not the outcome. Each step counts, and each step gets you closer to the finish line.

The Bottom Line

In this chapter, you have discovered how to expand your confidence through taking appropriate action. Free of doubt, you have learned to reach for challenging goals and take the necessary steps to make them happen. Acknowledging your internal and external obstacles, accepting them for what they are, and not making them mean something they don't frees you to act effectively. Lack of motivation and procrastination no longer has to interfere with success. Give yourself credit for taking action, which means not only identifying your accomplishments but also praising your efforts. Credit is in the doing and not just in the outcome. Getting in the game is what counts.

Chapter Eight

Maintain Your Confidence

The key to confidence comes from believing in yourself. Picture traveling through an imaginary day in which self-doubt no longer exists. Without doubt, calm takes over; in control, you confidently navigate the day.

Because you know you are competent, you are not rattled by problems, stressors, or hassles. You feel liberated and empowered because you are sure you can tackle anything. You can proceed at you own speed instead of being concerned that you are not working hard enough, accomplishing enough, setting the bar high enough, or doing well enough. You don't worry that your performance will be viewed by others as falling short. You know that you are competent and intelligent and can work at your own speed.

Knowing you are a desirable person, regardless of what any individual person on the planet has to say about it or what he or she does, frees you to enjoy life without interpersonal concerns.

Released from doubt, your confidence reigns. You are not constantly wondering if someone likes you, worrying about what others think, stewing over a disagreement, or thinking about whether someone is going to call you back or include you in his or her plans.

Self-doubt may whisper from time to time, but it no longer cripples you. You now know that your doubt stems from an inaccurate view of yourself. Based on the systematic program outlined in this book, you have identified your doubt label and its origins and have learned how to question and examine doubt for accuracy when it gets activated. You are also able to identify and modify your unspoken if/then rules and messages, understand how they developed, and replace them with more realistic and healthy rules and messages to live by. You're able to deconstruct your doubt label and build a more realistic confidence belief. You are a multifaceted, complex composite of many positive characteristics. You know how to take effective action. You're aware of the typical behavioral strategies that you tend to overuse and overgeneralize in response to most situations, and you have learned effective strategies for problem solving, developing goals, and planning an effective strategy of action. Lack of motivation and procrastination no longer hinder your performance or social interactions. You now know that you can count on yourself!

Deactivate Your Buttons So They Don't Get Pushed

There may still be times when your doubt erupts, and life is seen through a negative lens. Although confidence is becoming your new identity, minor events can push your buttons. A passing comment, a certain look, or seemingly innocuous behavior can activate

your doubt. Doubt comes from your interpretation of these inno-
cent events rather than from the event itself. When these events are
seen through your doubt filter, you become distressed and your old
overused behavioral strategies emerge. The activated doubt messages now get in your way.

You can keep your doubt buttons from getting pushed by knowing where you are vulnerable and by actively deciding to not let the
doubt win. When your doubt button gets activated, acknowledge
it as doubt; accept that it is still inside of you and that doubt is
just a global, derogatory, invalid label; and take appropriate action
by not letting it get in your way. Keep in mind that you've spent
years of listening to your doubt and it's hard to tune it out. If you
keep on recognizing your old doubt, rethinking it, and rewriting
to mirror reality, your confidence belief will gradually become
fortified and strengthened. Rehearsing your confidence belief will
allow it to reign. Your confidence belief is the accurate, realistic,
multicharacteristic composite of the true, updated, current you.

By using the four-step approach presented in this book to
squash doubt and build confidence, you not only know what your
buttons are but how to stop reacting or resorting to old behavioral
strategies when they get pressed. The key is to learn and consistently apply these strategies so that you are prepared when your
buttons get pushed. The steps put you back in the driver's seat,
with renewed confidence in your abilities. To help you deal with
your doubt buttons, keep the following points in mind:

- Your doubt label is an inaccurate, overgeneralized, self-depre-
  cating name that is absolutely never 100 percent globally true.

- Your doubt button is more likely to get pressed when you are
  under duress.

- Don't fall back into old thinking patterns. Recognize the button and the doubt it activated, rethink it, and rewrite it.

- Your confidence belief is the accurate, realistic, multicharacteristic composite of the true, updated, current you.

- Examine and problem solve the situation before your doubt button gets pressed.

Stress Can Reactivate Doubt

Stress is a normal part of daily life. Unfortunately, stress can reactivate doubt because the doubt may never be totally gone. We hope that you are successfully squashing doubt using the approach in this book. However, there may be some lingering doubt lying dormant waiting for stress to activate it. That's why it is so important to continue to do the work that you started while reading this book. By using your new skills, you can recognize doubt and see it for what it is, so doubt does not get the best of you. Doubt can be like a weed that under the right conditions pops up in the middle of your beautiful garden. Your job is to keep pulling it out no matter how many times it grows.

Stress does not have to get the best of you. Emotions color any situation and often lead you to see your stressors in an exaggerated way. You magnify the trouble and overestimate the probability of its negative consequences. Instead, realistically evaluate the worst, best, and most likely outcome and then realistically examine the internal and external assets you have developed to cope with the stress. Remember that your greatest asset is confidence. Confidence arms you to face any stressor because it lets you know that you have what it takes to cope. It's time to say *I can,* not *I can't.*

To keep stress from reactivating doubt, remember:

- Doubt can surface and distort the picture in a negative way.

- Just because doubt surfaces does not make the doubt label true.

- Don't let emotions color the situation.

- Realistically examine your stressor.

- Recognize that you have lots of internal and external assets available to you.

- It's time to say I *can*.

Gain Confidence Even if You Don't Fully Believe It

Often your brain grasps the compelling information in support of your confidence beliefs but your emotions still feel your doubt is valid. Your logical, rational brain needs to convince your irrational, emotional side that your doubts are wrong. As you learned in Chapter 6, one way to do this is to remind yourself of all the fact-driven logic that supports your confidence belief. Another way to continue to build your confidence and keep your feelings in check is to keep a confidence log.

The Confidence Log

Confidence logs are filled with daily recordings of experience, feedback, problem solving, and coping that fortify your confidence belief. Logs are intended to filter in the positive information and move you away from the old habit of unknowingly looking for negative information to confirm your doubt. Although you can be creative, there are two main types of logs: general and specific. A general log is an overall reflection of performance and/or social success. People often name their general logs something like Feel Good About Me Log, I'm Okay Log, or I Can Cope Log. A specific log where you keep a record of data that specifically addresses your clearly identified confidence belief. This type of log directly links to your individual self-doubt by looking for data to confirm the alternative new positive confidence belief. You might title your log with one of these: I'm Adequate Log, I'm Strong Log, I'm an Attractive Package Log, I'm Likable Log, I'm Desirable Log, I'm Capable Log, I'm Competent Log, I'm Successful Log, I'm Smart Log, or I'm a Good Person Log. For examples, see Sam's and Jill's logs.

Sam's I'm Competent Log

Thursday

- Made a substantial sale.

- Set limits with my daughter.

- Was assertive with my mother.

- Handled a difficult situation with my administrative assistant regarding her hours.

- Played a great round of golf.

Friday

- Got almost everything done on my to-do list.

- Was assertive with mom once again.

- Left work at a reasonable time.

- Handled all the arrangements for mom's transportation.

- Organized a foursome for Saturday's golf game.

Saturday

- Didn't lose my cool when my golf game started out poorly.

- Negotiated a good price on a new washing machine and dryer.

- Won big at cards.

- Got the virus off my computer without any help.

- Beat the computer at Texas Hold 'Em.

Conclusion

- There are lots of data to support my competency. I *am* competent!

Jill's I'm Loved Log

Thursday

- Maria asked me to join her and some friends to go dancing.

- My aunt told me how special I am.

- My sister thanked me for helping her out.

- I was complimented on my outfit.

- My relatives asked me if they could stay with me because they have liked staying with me better than with anyone else.

Friday

- Maria begged me to join them when I said I might not go dancing.

- My cats would not leave my side and seemed happy to be cuddled.

- My niece asked me to be her special guest at an event at her school.

Saturday

- My date told me how much he enjoyed our evening.

- My mom told me dinner last Sunday was not the same without me and how happy she was that I was coming tomorrow.

- My sister called unexpectedly just to be nice.

Conclusion

- People do care about me and do want me in their lives. I *am* lovable!

Create your own confidence log. You can do this on paper or on your computer. Start by giving it a title. For a specific log, you'd use an "I am" statement. Collect data every day. Every few days look at the data you collected and make your conclusions clear. The fact that what you recorded actually happened means your new confident view of yourself is valid. Record it, review it, and write out the conclusions, allowing your confidence to grow and be reinforced.

Acting Confident

Often seeing is believing, so if you want to *be* confident, try *acting* confident. Acting confident means moving through your day as if you fully believed the confident view of yourself were the truth. Try it out for a day, a week, or the rest of your life.

Consider Pat. Pat has left a large company to start his own business, and although it is growing, it is not generating the revenue he had hoped. Reflecting back to his college days, he remembers struggling in school and his parents continually asking why he couldn't get better grades. His old doubt of being a failure pops up every time he looks at the numbers in his account. The facts are that he actually is a success: He has successfully launched his business, it is growing, it is paying his bills, and it has provided him with his dream of flexibility and freedom. Despite the facts, he still feels like that failure.

For Pat, acting confident is waking up with the confidence belief "I am a success." Instead of wanting to roll over when the alarm goes off early in the morning, he gets right out of bed feeling good about himself. While brushing his teeth, he thinks about how much he has accomplished. He looks at the large flat-screen television and sees it as a measure of his success. Heading off to the office, he is happy to have work and is not wondering how he will get it all done; he plans strategically to tackle the day. He arrives at the office, knowing it is his and that the work to do is evidence of his success. He smiles, completely aware that he made it all happen. Leaving work, he rushes to his kid's soccer game. Standing on the sidelines next to his wife, with his younger son in his arms, he smiles at the success of his life. Arriving home, the family jokes with each other and giggles as they prepare for bed. Pat climbs into bed and peacefully falls asleep, accepting that he is a success.

Now let's take a look at Chris. Chris continues to feel like an unattractive person despite the facts: She's a runner whose body is tone and fit, a woman with an endless list of jokes and a good sense of humor, a gifted student who was awarded an academic scholarship that paid for her schooling, and a gourmet cook. Plus, her boyfriend adores her. Her doubt label that she is unattractive stems from her belief that she was a chubby child who was shy and reluctant to initiate friendships. In addition, she grew up with a mother who was devoted to her family who had few friends. Her mother was a poor role model for social success, leaving Chris without the skills needed to feel comfortable in a social world.

The belief that she is unattractive is perpetuated every time her emails go unanswered or her phone calls are not returned. Chris labors over every word she writes and every word she says when communicating with friends, believing that if she does not get it right, they will not want to be her friend. After deciding to try acting confident, Chris wakes up with the courage to plan a dinner party and invite people over. That morning, she looks in the mirror as she gets dressed and finally notices her beautiful smile and the clearness of her complexion. She makes a joke and laughs out loud to herself, realizing that she is funny. Instead of keeping her humor to herself, she calls a friend and shares the joke. She takes the opportunity to invite that woman and her boyfriend over for dinner that very night. Encouraged by her friend's acceptance, she calls another friend. With no concern for how she is communicating, she tentatively invites another couple. Getting dressed for the evening, Chris puts on her favorite jeans and finally allows herself to see the fit figure she has worked hard to maintain. Confident that her friends will find her entertaining, she starts preparing the meal in a good mood. She spontaneously hugs her boyfriend and tells him he looks great; she feels good about herself without needing reassurance from him. She enjoys herself during the dinner, fully participating in the moment without concern that she is saying or behaving inappropriately. Saying good-bye to her friends and cleaning up with her boyfriend, she realizes she has many qualities that make her an attractive person.

In both of these examples of acting confident, evidence existed to support confidence even though neither person truly felt it before trying it. By acting confident, Pat and Chris were able to embrace a positive view of themselves. In fact, it helped them strengthen their confidence. Their feelings were now aligned with the facts. Remember: Even if doesn't feel true, it doesn't mean it isn't true.

ACTING CONFIDENT EXERCISE

1. Name your confidence belief.

2. List some of the characteristics that support your confidence belief.

3. Embrace those characteristics as you act confident.

Maintaining Your Confidence

Don't take your confidence for granted. Like any asset, it needs to be nurtured. Maintaining your confidence means continuing to strengthen your confidence belief. Be your own personal trainer. Regularly exercise your brain so that confidence does not deteriorate. By retraining your brain to look for the positives, you flex and strengthen your confidence muscle. This also helps weaken doubt so that over time it atrophies.

Use the following checklist so that you can make sure you are putting yourself through the full circuit of exercises. Keep practicing the skills, and over time, they will become a more natural part of how you see yourself and the world. If you struggle, review the checklist to identify where you are struggling and review the appropriate skill.

Think Confident, Be Confident Checklist

- Record your personality style.

- Label your doubt.

- Record life experiences that have shaped your doubt.

- When confronted with a stressor: write down the activating situation (A) and record your body response (B), cognitions (C), doubt (D), and emotions (E) in response to that situation in your Doubt Register. It's as easy as ABC.

- Determine whether you are experiencing a realistic concern or doubt.

- Logically and objectively examine the facts (F). Record them in your Doubt Register.

- Take a timed time-out if your emotions are too intense so you can move from emotional thinking to logical thinking.

- Realistically understand your vulnerability in comparison to your internal and external assets.

- Stick with the facts so you can take the power away from doubt; it's go time: rethink, relax, and respond effectively (G). Record these facts in your Doubt Register.

- Remember doubt filters information from the environment in a distorted way, which leads you to draw faulty conclusions, which in turn build and perpetuate the doubt.

- Remove the distortion filter so you can see the whole picture.

- Remove rigid positive and negative if/then rules and the messages that stem from doubt.

- Don't get trapped into using old, overused behavioral strategies.

- Write down and use your multiple, new, adaptive behavioral strategies.

- Write down and use your new confidence-building rules.

- Continue to develop and strengthen each new confidence belief.

- Don't focus on the snapshot; run the whole tape to get the real deal.

- Build and strengthen each confidence belief by adding to your list of assets.

- When in distress, use the three As: acknowledge, accept, act.

- Problem solve: List your options, examine each one, choose one or several that seem to be the best fit, and then follow your plan of action.

- To reach your goals: plan, take action, and have a rationale.

- Go for it rather than give up; stop procrastination.

- Remind yourself that motivation comes from taking action.

- Give yourself credit for both the effort and the accomplishments.

- Know your buttons so they don't get pushed.

- Recognize that stress can activate your doubt. Use your skills to defeat the doubt, and use your confidence to face the stress.

- Keep your confidence log.

- Try acting confident even when you don't fully believe it.

The Bottom Line

Carry your new perspective into your day, incorporate it into how you live your life and the choices you make. Now that you are free from doubt and are living with confidence, take the opportunity to live life to the fullest. Try to remember your hopes and dreams and the opportunities that you may have once dismissed; now's the time to go for it. Confidence is your new *can do* attitude.

YOUR OWN DOUBT REGISTER

ACTIVATING SITUATION (YOU)	BODY RESPONSE	COGNITIONS	DOUBT LABEL	EMOTION	FACTS	GO TIME: RETHINK, RELAX, RESPOND

ACTIVATING SITUATION (YOU)	BODY RESPONSE	COGNITIONS	DOUBT LABEL	EMOTION	FACTS	GO TIME: RETHINK, RELAX, RESPOND

ACTIVATING SITUATION (YOU)	BODY RESPONSE	COGNITIONS	DOUBT LABEL	EMOTION	FACTS	GO TIME: RETHINK, RELAX, RESPOND

ACTIVATING SITUATION (YOU)	BODY RESPONSE	COGNITIONS	DOUBT LABEL	EMOTION	FACTS	GO TIME: RETHINK, RELAX, RESPOND

ACTIVATING SITUATION (YOU)	BODY RESPONSE	COGNITIONS	DOUBT LABEL	EMOTION	FACTS	GO TIME: RETHINK, RELAX, RESPOND

ACKNOWLEDGMENTS

A huge thank you to our children, Chad, Alex, and Max Detweiler and Jesse, Ethan, and Carly Fox, for being our greatest fans and cheerleaders. Extra-special thanks to our husbands, Robert Detweiler and Stuart Fox, for providing lots of help both with the book and with keeping our households glued together during this journey.

We are so fortunate to have wonderful family and friends who all pitched in to help make this book happen. We are indebted to Doris Schwartz and Jodi Sokol for their countless hours of expert editing and thoughtful suggestions and to Marvin S. Gittes and Liane Browne for their many hours of legal assistance. Thanks also to Mark Likness for his computer expertise. We are grateful for the support of Phyllis and Arnold Sokol, Marc Sokol, Stephen Schwartz, Margaret Gittes, and Alvin and Esther Fox. Thank you to Geri and James Davis and Tech Commandos for making our website happen. We would like to thank Janet Stratt, Tina Lizzio, Sharon Feltingoff, Laurie Solakian, and Helaine Leibowitz for their encouragement and editorial comments and for making it so that our children did not notice how hard we were working. Special appreciation to our dear friends and colleagues Chris Reilly and Shelley Milestone. Finally, we'd like to thank our patients and supervisees who continually inspire us.

We are extremely grateful to Anne Marie O'Farrell, our agent, for believing in us right from the start and expertly guiding us throughout this process. We greatly appreciate our extremely talented editor, Meg Leder, who shared our vision and shaped our book to its improvement. Thank you also to Beth Leiberman for helping us write a strong proposal and outline a clear path for our manuscript. We also want to thank Jennifer Eck and her team for smoothly coordinating each step in this process.

We are indebted to the Beck Institute staff, especially Julie Snow Regan, Bonnie Villari, and Marina Stamos for their undying support and assistance. Special thanks to Naomi Dank who can make anything happen.

We would especially like to thank Drs. Judith and Aaron T. Beck for their inspiration and guidance. Aaron T. Beck enlightened us with his world-shattering cognitive therapy model, and we remain his loyal devotees.

INDEX

ABOUT THE AUTHORS

Leslie Sokol, PhD, is a licensed psychologist and distinguished founding fellow, past president, treasurer, and credentials chair in the Academy of Cognitive Therapy. She is the director of education at the Beck Institute for Cognitive Therapy and Research, lectures nationally and internationally, and maintains a private practice in the Philadelphia suburbs.

Marci G. Fox, PhD, is a licensed psychologist and founding fellow in the Academy of Cognitive Therapy who also serves on its board of examiners. She is a senior faculty member in the extramural training program at the Beck Institute for Cognitive Therapy and Research and maintains a private practice in Boca Raton, Florida.

To arrange a speaking engagement for Leslie Sokol, PhD, and Marci G. Fox, PhD, please contact the Penguin Speakers Bureau at speakersbureau@us.penguingroup.com